Baby's first year

A Complete guide on what to expect from your first parenting year – Including baby sleep, baby food recipes, baby games, and your baby's cognitive development

Contents

Introduction

The first year of your baby's life is definitely an exciting and awe-inspiring time. You will see your baby growing with each passing day. She might be cranky at times, and joyful at others, and the new developments will keep on happening as weeks pass.

As a new parent, this could be quite a prodigious task to take care of. You will be busy taking care of your baby, while also adoring her at the same time.

If the whole task seems a bit overwhelming to you, here is a well-compiled guide that will walk you through all the important developments that you can expect in the first year.

Right from her first days, to taking care of bathing and skin care and comforting her and understanding her temperament, this guide covers all the important elements that you must know about.

Let's get started.

Entering Into the Parenthood:
Baby's First Days

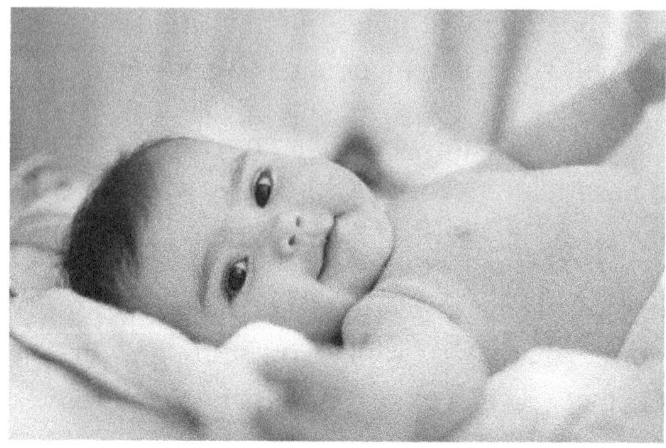

Since labor and delivery are processes that are exhausting for both mother and baby, it affects their overall health drastically. While mothers feel exhausted and completely drained, the infants experience a little pain, slight deformation and complete exposure to a new world.

A lot of babies cry a lot on their first days because either there's too much light in the room or the room temperature is very different from the temperature inside the womb. Parents and doctors need to ensure that the baby is kept under proper protection against heat and cold.

Doctor's urge mothers to feed their baby as soon as they are born because it adds to their immunity and emotional support system. The process of breastfeeding is more of an emotional connection than a physical one. With the milk, a lot of enzymes are transferred that improve immunity and add to the trust. The overall development of the support system makes it easier for the kid to rely on the mother and become calm.

A lot of important processes like tests, vaccination, and breastfeeding should be combined to leverage the kid with the development of the requisite immune and support system.

Let's learn more about the kind of deformation a baby suffers during delivery

- Pointy Head

Millions of parents have gone on record and mentioned that their kid was born with a pointed head. Well! No baby actually inherits a pointy head, it's just that the head turns slightly pointed because they cross crevices while coming out of the mother's womb. The deformation is temporary and has no diverse effects on the health of the baby.

The slight deformation actually assists delivery and saves the mother a lot of pain. With the head turning pointy, it gets easier for the kid to come out. Also, the pointy head turns back to the round shape in less than 2 weeks.

One of the best ways to get rid of a pointy head is to massage it gently with olive oil. With gentle massage on a daily basis, the head will get back into shape and will also have the requisite strength.

- The baby appears to be scrunched up

Since your baby has spent around 9 months into the womb, where space is restricted, their body bends in a particular shape. During the first few days after delivery, babies have a shape that looks more like an oval disc.

Scrunched up shape is not something to worry about because it is common and happens with every full-grown baby. In case, babies are prematurely delivered, they might have straight bodies but then they need additional medical support. With the help of regular massage and activities, the babies get into their original shape quite easily.

- Paper thin nails and fragile toes

In case, you notice that your newborn has paper thin nails and fragile toes, do not panic, it has got nothing to do with the health of your baby. A baby is generally healthy until mentioned by the doctors even if they have paper thin nails and fragile toes. Since the baby has spent a lot of time inside the womb, where it is all wet and greasy, these nails and toes appear to be thin and fragile. With time, they will get back into shape and will have the requisite strength and shine.

- The skin appears to be purple

If your baby is born with a white, red or purple skin, do not panic because it is pretty normal. The real color starts to appear only after a few days after being exposed to the real world. Doctors might suggest you wash off the vernix to get rid of the extremely red or purple color.

- Rashes and blotches

These are normal and happen with almost every baby. These rashes and blotches clear up under 24 hours generally. However, if the rashes and blotches remain even after a week, get in touch with a doctor for examination.

- The shape and overall appearance change every week

As your baby continues to grow, her body stretches out and the overall shape starts improving. With every massage, your baby will grow strong and with every day, it will grow bigger. Do not be scared or panic if your baby grows slowly, till the time their reports are clear, you need not worry.

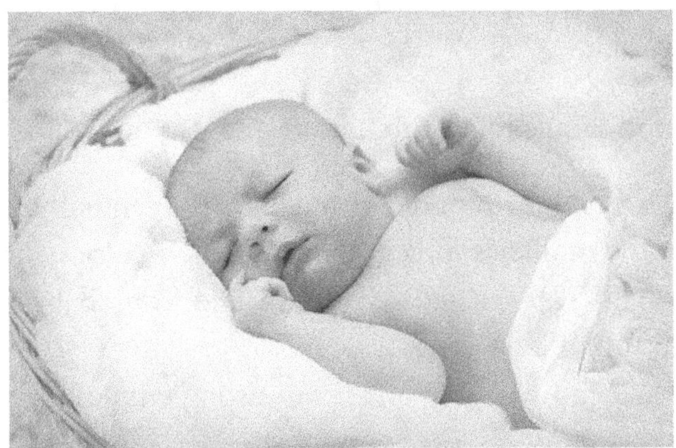

Now that it is clear that all those rashes and blotches are temporary and will clear out on their own, you need to stop worrying about your baby's appearance and instead, concentrate on her health.

- Birthmarks

These are temporary and occur because of being scrunched in the womb, they will clear out on their own within a few weeks. You do not need to worry about them, sometimes a little blotch will last forever but those are cute memories.

- Facial appearance

There's no guarantee that your baby will remain as red or pink as they appeared on the first day. Over the days and weeks, her color and facial appearance will change, it should not astound you. Though all these changes are normal and happen with every baby, you must understand that it is out of your control. With more hair coming and more blotches clearing up, your baby will become more beautiful on a daily basis, rejoice it.

A huge percentage of babies are born bald and there's nothing wrong with that. Babies from around the world are born with bald patches that heal over the weeks.

Some common things related to hair in infants you will notice:

- The hair might be golden but it will eventually gain protein from the mother's milk and change their color
- The bald patches will cover up and your baby will have a scalp full of hair
- The hair fall will stop and grow strong with every passing day

Bonding With Your Baby

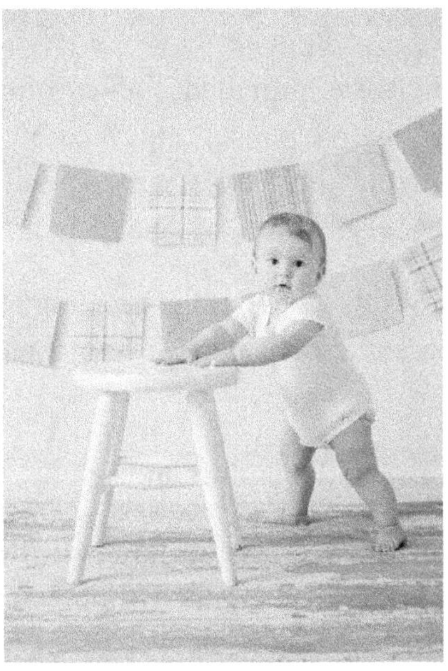

While the actual development of a baby happens during the nine months of pregnancy, she starts getting accustomed to the earth's atmosphere only after delivery. Once into the real world, the baby might take a few days to adjust with the surroundings, lighting and other important things like response, sensibility, and reflexes.

A baby's first few days are more about regular checkups and self-development. While parents and doctors must always look around for symptoms of varied diseases but the baby must also be provided with its time to rest and adjust to the real world.

A lot of studies conducted on monkeys and their newborn infants have shown that early stage bonding makes the baby healthier, better behaved and quite smart.

The purpose of these studies was to find out whether the bonding of babies with parents has any effect on their overall mental and physical health or not. The studies have shown signs that early stage bonding is very important because it shapes the brain in a particular way.

Infants of monkeys were provided the comfort of fake monkey mothers to register the response, the fake monkey was equally comfortable and soft but the babies who actually bonded with real mothers were way better behaved, agile and smart.

Now this clearly shows that early stage bonding is important, here are few things every parent should keep in mind while bonding with a newborn baby:

- No compromise with comfort and safety

A lot of family members will line up to meet the newborn, but as a parent, you should decide how much time your baby is going to spend with them. Stand by your baby and ensure that everyone is handling your baby better and firmly.

Newborn babies can experience body deformation, hence it is important to not move around with them in your arms. Put them on a flat surface ensuring requisite comfort and agility. While movement should be restricted, it is also necessary to ensure that the infant is comfortable at the room temperature.

- Hand sanitizers are life savers

Well! You can rule out 99% chances of infection if everyone who gets close to the kid uses hand sanitizer before touching them. Newborn kids are very sensitive to infections and bacteria. Any chance that you take will lead to lethal problems. Just by relying on a medically proven hand sanitizer, you can safeguard your kid from all kinds of bacteria and viruses.

- Not too much light

Since a newborn baby sees the light for the first time only after delivery, it is necessary for the parents to ensure that they are not being exposed to a lot of light. A room full of light just might not be the right place for your newborn.

Either pull the curtains, dim the light or request the hospital staff to put your baby in a room designed for newborn infants. She will get used to the light slowly. Do not rush the process, as this way, you might even end up damaging her pupils.

Parents need to be highly attentive and available for their baby, any mistake can either lead to infection or lethal diseases, be extra careful or protect them against popular viruses that transmit through touch and air.

Babies bond aggressively after birth while parents take time. A lot of parents are scared and perhaps this is why they are skeptical about taking the first few steps towards bonding. While parents are scared, it is completely normal for kids to bond aggressively, they will touch you, hold your hand and also grab anything they can lay their hands on.

Some of the common ways in which a kid reaches out to his or her parents for bonding immediately after birth are:

- Touch

Undoubtedly the easiest way and the first language of communication. While parents adore the touches of a newborn infant, the babies find it soothing and comforting. Studies have shown that kids who are provided with instant bonding after birth are easy to manage and do not cry much. Varied studies and significant data hints that better bonding can help you raise good kids and better human beings.

Also, it is important for parents to ensure that every touch is safe and secure. Make use of hand sanitizers aggressively, and ensure proper safety of your baby.

- Eye to eye communication

While touch is soothing, eye to eye communication promotes trust. Kids understand that the following person is safe and is here to comfort them. More and more eye connect tends to comfort the kids emotionally and stops them from crying.

A baby that receives good eye to eye communication in his or her early days will grow into a calm and a person who trusts others. Studies have proved that touch and eye to eye contact when mixed properly can help babies sleep easily and cry less.

- Facial expressions and gestures

Since babies cannot speak, they tend to express their feelings through facial expressions and gestures and most of these expressions and gestures are a simple imitation of you. Parents can easily observe that their baby is making similar expressions during the early days.

When it comes to the newborn baby, the all communication that matters is with her mother. A mother's touch, eye to eye contact, breastfeeding and cuddling will assure the kid like no other. The mother must be allowed to interact with her baby on the very first day to help the baby calm down and have the requisite comfort.

What are the best ways of bonding between the mother and the newborn?

- Breast feeding

There's no better way than a mother feeding her baby. This not only calms her down but also helps her build the requisite trust. It has been scientifically proven in humans as well as in other animals, that breastfeeding is the best way to bond with a newborn. Doctors also urge mothers to feed their baby on the very first day. Since mother's milk provides a baby with the requisite nutrients, they become more relaxed, calm, and strong and it stops them from crying.

On the very first day, the baby needs more strength to adjust to the room temperature, lighting, atmosphere, and human touches, hence breastfeeding is important.

Bathing a newborn can seem difficult and tricky at first, but if handled with little preparation and setup, baby's first bath could be joyful and a great stress-free experience. For a newborn baby, it is recommended to sponge-bath instead of a proper bath for a few days.

Baby's umbilical cord stump takes at least 10 days to fall off and it is best to sponge bath your baby to avoid making the cord stump wet. Give your baby a gentle and quick sponge bath for a few days after birth:

Here's how you can sponge bathe newly born:

- Keep supplies handy

Gather baby bath supplies like a dry towel, clean diaper, and sponge and running water basin. Make sure they are within one arm distance so that you don't have to step away even for a second.

- Pick a warm place

Choose a warm spot for baby's bath. It could be a baby bathtub or sink, see that it's comfortable for you to kneel or stand with one hand always on the baby. Use a flat and soft surface to lay the baby.

- One section at a time

Gently wipe the baby all over by using a washcloth or sponge dipped in warm water. Keep your baby wrapped and wash one section at a time. Wash one limb while the other is covered. Pat dry before you start with the next limb.

- How often should you bathe a newly born?

Sponge bathing your baby one to three days a week is enough. It is not necessary to bath them every day. Of course, the diaper area should be cleaned and, you can wipe her neck and knees as well. For older babies, it can be as much as every day as they start crawling and getting into places.

- The big bath

Once the umbilical cord stump dries up and falls off, the baby is ready for the big bath. You can start with a tub bath every few days once the area heals. Some parents bathe their baby every day, however, it is not necessary until your baby starts getting down and dirty on the ground. Bathing too often can dry up the skin so, 2-3 times a week should be good.

You might want to get help from your partner or a family member. It's best to have caregivers nearby during early baths and you will need extra hands to hold on your little slippery one. After you have gathered all the supplies for the baby's bath, follow the below steps and get started:

- Step 1

Fill a few inches of warm water in the bathtub. 2-3 inches of warm water in the tub is enough to keep baby safe. The bath temperature should be 90-100 degrees Fahrenheit. As babies catch a cold easily, the water should be warmer than you would expect but not hot.

- Step 2

Undress your little one and gently slide your baby in the warm water, feet first. Make sure that you don't put the baby in the bathtub while the water is still running. Use one hand to support the neck and head all the time. Pour bath water over the baby regularly so that they don't get cold.

- Step 3

Keep the baby covered as they can easily lose heat. So, try to keep them covered with a warm washcloth. You can switch the cloth with a fresh warm washcloth in intervals. Switch on the thermostat so that the house is warmer, and the baby doesn't feel cold during and after the bath.

- Step 4

Use mild soap and use less of it as it can make baby's skin dry. Take a wet soapy cloth and gently start with her scalp, then clean eyes and face. If mucus has dried near nose and eyes, dab it two times to soften it and wipe it out.

- Step 5

Pour a cupful of water and wipe her thoroughly with a clean washcloth. Pay special attention to areas having creases like arms, behind ears, around the neck and genital area. Very carefully, take your baby out of the bathtub with one hand supporting neck and head and the other supporting bottom. Babies are slippery when they are wet.

- Step 6

Wrap your baby in a dry soft hooded towel and pat her dry. It is not necessary to apply lotions and powders after baby's wash as it is generally the dead skin that comes off. You can apply mild moisturizer or coconut oil on dry patches. Diaper her, dress her and give your sweet-smelling little one a kiss on the forehead.

Some Tips for Bathing Your Baby

- Stay safe

Never leave a baby alone in the bathtub even for a moment. You need to have at least one hand on the baby all the time. It is best you have your partner nearby when giving a bath to your baby.

- Don't force

If your baby absolutely hates bathing in a tub, go for sponge days for few more days until the baby is comfortable enough for the bathtub.

- Use soap sparingly

Use a mild soap for diaper area and the rest of the body can be wiped down using water and washcloth. Too much soap irritates skin and dries it up.

- Shampoo hair with tear-free baby shampoo

If she has hair, use a tiny bit of shampoo and lather your baby's scalp. Message with your fingers and be very gentle. Gently rinse wipe off with a washcloth.

- Go easy with baby products and avoid powder

Powder particles can get into the lungs of the baby and cause respiratory problems. It is always recommended to avoid powder. And that beautiful sensitive skin doesn't need much lotion and products. Babies are already sweet smelling. Use coconut oil to nourish if required.

Parents develop a special bond with the baby while bathing them. Of course, there's a lot to think and take care of when it comes to bathing your little one but soon enough, you will be a pro. And before you know it, your child will be sitting in the bathtub on its own splashing water and enjoying that bath.

You can potty train your baby as a part of the natural infant hygiene y. Even though at this age, babies will probably be using diapers and once they grow older, at about eighteen months they will themselves be able to figure out when to go to the potty.

However, if your baby is potty trained then she will be more comfortable, especially if she is not used to wearing diapers for longer periods of time.

Also, as they start growing, babies will start developing motor skills and will be more active so instead of changing their diaper constantly, they can be encouraged to use the potty.

Now, infant potty training is not a very easy process and there is bound to happen a few accidents on the way. If this happens, make sure that you have supplies ready to clean your baby because it will be distressing for her.

Following are some tips that should be kept in mind when you start potty training your infant.

- Observe your baby and figure out her elimination schedules. Try to keep track of how many times your baby needs to use the toilet and also if she gives any signs, however subtle, before she needs to go. These signs might be expressions or sounds or even gestures.
- When you take your baby to the bathroom, always keep a small bucket or even a pot and hold her over it. This will allow you to introduce your baby to her own potty which will be small enough to suit her.
- Talk to your baby while she is relieving herself. Often babies associate a particular sound or expression with elimination, so this will make it easier to engage your baby's attention.

- Keep repeating the sound or expression whenever you see that your baby has to go and she will soon come to identify this as a signal that will connect with her urge to go to the potty.

- Infant potty training can often take a long time and each baby learns differently. So do not put any pressure on your baby while training her. Instead, make sure that your baby is comfortable using the potty and is feeling good about it.

- Sometimes none of this might work and your baby might not want to use her own potty and might make a fuss. During such times, stay calm and soothe your baby if she is frantic. Once your baby is relaxed, be patient and try the training later, at a different time.

- Do not be very strict when it comes to training your infant to use the potty. Babies deal with hygiene training better if the patterns are flexible and you should ease your baby into a particular schedule. Therefore it is completely alright if you want to occasionally use a diaper, especially at night.

The umbilical cord has formed the best connection between you and the baby during your pregnancy days to transport nutrients from you to the little one. Now, it is time to take care of the one-inch stump that will take some time to dry and fall off.

But, taking care of it is of utmost importance at this point since this can lead to infections and irritations in the newborn baby. Here are some ideas by which you can take care of the umbilical cord.

- Keep the cord area clean

The first and most important aspect of taking care of the umbilical cord is to keep it clean. This means you would have to clean the base of the cord. The best method would be to use rubbing alcohol.

But doctors, off late, tend to avoid that owing to the skin irritations it can cause. However, there are always some alternative methods that can be adopted in order to keep the area clean. It is best to consult your pediatrician for that!

- Keep the cord area dry

The idea is to help the baby's umbilical cord heal faster. In that regard, it would be a good idea to keep that area open and exposed to air in order to let it dry. Some baby diapers have a special design where the diapers can be folded downwards. This will give the umbilical cord stump a better chance to dry and heal.

Also, during the summer months, it would be best to keep the newborn baby dressed in only a t-shirt and diapers in order to keep the area open. These are some ideas by which you could help the drying process.

- Give sponge baths to your baby

With the piece of the umbilical cord still attached to the baby, they are indeed in a very sensitive phase. You cannot risk the chance of rubbing the cord off, even by mistake. Thus, it would be a good idea to not give the baby a full bath in a tub. That will bring up the additional problem of rubbing the body dry.

If you have to provide a tub bath, it would be a good idea to just fan the area until it is completely dry. As an alternative solution, you could also give sponge baths to the baby till such time the cord does not fall off.

- Let the cord heal naturally

Sometimes it might happen that the remains of the umbilical cord might just be hanging by a thread on the body of the baby. In these situations, sometimes the parents are tempted to just pull or pluck it out of the body in order to remove chances of infection. But that could be a really bad idea.

This, in fact, might lead to bigger issues. Instead, it is a better idea to allow the cord to heal naturally, on its own, taking its own time. This gives a better healing environment to the body as well.

How to Detect Infections with the Umbilical Cord?

A lot of new parents are actually unaware of the possibility of infections related to the umbilical cord. Yes, it is a natural process and the remains are likely to come off within a couple of weeks, but in those few days as well, the newborn could develop an infection. And some of these could be very harmful to the body.

For instance, a common umbilical cord infection is called omphalitis can prove to be a life-threatening infection. This also requires immediate treatment. Hence, to be on the safe side, it is best to take a few protections against such infections and be wary of certain symptoms.

If the base of the umbilical cord appears to be red or swollen, then it is bad news for the baby and the parents. In all probability, it signals an imminent infection.

A bleeding umbilical cord is not a good sight at all. This could again be an indication of an infection coming your way. This should be checked by the doctor immediately.

Sometimes, the cord gives rise to some pus formation which could be very detrimental for the baby's health. This could be yellowish or white in color and could be oozing out from near the cord area.

Apart from the pus, if you notice a discharge given out from the healing zone, you could get it checked. At times, this discharge could be accompanied by a foul smell. Even though it might feel like something very unimportant, it could be the start of a bad infection.

If your newborn baby is reacting adversely to the umbilical cord and appears to be in some sort of pain, this might not be going the right way. This also requires immediate attention because the baby might be incapable of expressing the pain while the infection is building up.

When Should You Call a Pediatrician?

With a newborn baby at home, you would naturally also be alert about their needs and issues. But when it comes to the umbilical cord, you are required to be extra cautious just so the process takes a natural course. When is it alarming enough to call up the pediatrician and ask for guidance? There are essentially two such criteria.

In the first situation, if you happen to notice signs of infection, your first point of action would be to call your doctor and apprise him of the condition. This essentially refers to all the signs of infection we mentioned previously.

Secondly, if the area is actively bleeding, it is again time to call the doctor. What exactly is active bleeding? This basically refers to a situation when there is a drop of blood in that area and when you wipe it off, another drop appears in the same region. This could possibly mean that the cord has come off prematurely or it has been pulled off for some reason. It is imperative to contact the doctor here and get your baby checked.

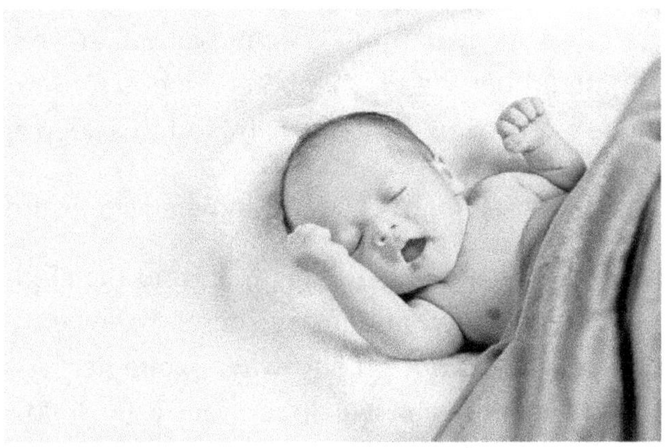

Newborns usually sleep a lot throughout the day and most of the time they do not sleep for a long time but wake in between for short periods of time. After a few weeks, your baby will slowly learn to distinguish between day and night and you can start regulating his/ her sleep schedule accordingly. Given below are some tips that's can help and establish a healthy sleeping pattern for your baby.

- Lie your baby down on the bed when she is a bit sleepy but not yet asleep

Newborns usually tend to be a bit drowsy once they've been breastfed as nursing calms them down. But often, during other times too they might feel sleepy and it is important to look for the signs because if a baby is sleepy then she will yawn occasionally and rub her eyes. If you notice this, then lay your baby down on the bed and soothe her while she slowly drifts off to sleep. Do not try to force a sleeping schedule, but wait your baby to nod off. Once babies grow older, this will develop the habit of drifting off to sleep on their own, once they lie down on the bed.

- Wait sometime before attending your baby if she is cooing or making soft sounds while sleeping.

Sometimes while sleeping, your baby might make soft cooing sounds but not fully awake. If this happens then do not immediately hold her or cuddle but allow your baby to soothe herself. If your baby does wake up, then attend her but do this before she is too frantic because other it will take a long time for your baby to fall asleep again.

- Do not catch your baby's attention when she is drowsy.

Babies often have the tendency to stay alert and the slightest activity can make them curious and attentive. Therefore, when your baby is sleepy, make sure you do not, in any way, excite her. Also, it should be kept in mind that this can be done simply by holding her gaze because it is usually a signal for playtime to your baby. So, do not make eye contact or have any direct interaction, other than sometimes rocking her to sleep or snuggling. Let your baby slowly drift off to sleep.

- Use the lights to regulate your baby's sleep patterns

If you are able to strategically use the electric lights and the natural light during the daytime then you can teach your baby the concept of day and night. During the day, if your baby is drowsy, make sure you are letting her sleep in a well-lit area. At night, dim the lights or use a night light that is soft and soothing and if your baby wakes up during the night, do not immediately switch on all lights, but try to calm her down and then drift off.

Babies cry as it is the only form or way in which they can communicate until they learn to speak eloquently. They usually cry for a few common reasons. Some babies cry their hearts out even for a change of diaper while some just whimper even when they are super hungry. Here are some of the reasons why babies cry so that the next time when your baby cries you know why.

- Hunger

Hunger is probably the foremost reason why your baby is crying. Even adults get cranky when they are hungry, think about how babies who can't even say they are hungry will react. It is better to learn to recognize the first signs babies show when they are hungry and well before their hunger turns into screams.

Babies have a habit of putting their hand in mouth, smacking their lips and, rooting when they are hungry. Research says when a baby cries out of hunger, there is a 'neh' sound that they produce while crying. So, next time when your baby cries do try to notice what sound they make while crying. That sounds like fun!

- Discomfort

Our discomfort can be due to anything be it a fallen eyelash in our eye, hair stuck around toe or cloth tag brushing with our skin. However, we are capable of eliminating our discomfort soon as we realize, unlike the newborns.

The only way they can convey their irritation and discomfort is through crying. If your baby continues to cry even after being fed, burped, napped and changed, the next thing you should do is strip down his clothes and see what is troubling her.

- Loneliness, boredom or fear

Yup, just like us they can also feel lonely at times when they have slept enough. If your baby is bored, she is likely to start crying to seek attention and in the want of someone to play with her.

In such cases, you should just hand her toys and she will start glowing with happiness again. Also, you take your baby out for a walk on the stroller, tell her father to play with her and rock her for a while or you can take her on a car ride. She will surely be delighted by any of these.

You must have definitely experienced this even if you are not a parent. If your baby starts crying in the middle of the night, it's probably due to a nightmare and out of fear. There is nothing to worry about in such situations. Sooth her and cuddle her close to you until she goes back to sleep.

- Overtiredness or overstimulation

Actually yes! Your baby can start crying because she was over enthusiastic the whole day and now super tired that she can't go back to sleep. Due to excessive activity, it may be that her legs are paining or she is feeling lethargic. The best thing to do in such cases is to make her sleep by singing her lullabies or anything that can distract her and provide her relief from tiredness. You can simply massage her legs and hands to make her feel better.

Over activity can lead to overstimulation when the baby gets continuously passed on from uncles to aunts to siblings to grandparents; it gets too much for her. All this commotion is new to her and she is still getting used to it. In such cases, it is good to allow her to rest for a while but doesn't completely ward her off from stimulation. Stimulation is a good thing for a baby.

- Colic

That's the last reason you would want your crying baby reason to be. Colic is referred to as a situation of severe pain in the abdomen due to obstruction in intestines. This is commonly prevalent in babies only.

A Colic child continues to cry for hours even when you are sure it is not for the reasons stated above. It is indeed difficult to console them and parenting can be one big task for the parents. But the good news is Colic is short lived. Also, often they are essentially not in pain, it is just their way to handle life as a baby. So no worries, this too shall pass. As parents just keep your cool and do not stress out.

- Teething

Being cranky for a child when their milk teeth are on their way is obvious. It can be painful for most babies as new tooth pushes their way out from the soft gums. This usually starts happening after around 4 to 7 months varying according to the child.

A gum massage can be of much help during teething. Babies while teething are more inclined to put their fists inside their mouth as this makes them feel better. Chewing on frozen teethers, washcloths, or cotton bibs also provide them relief. Try your best to provide the baby with natural relief rather than going for medications until the baby is in intolerable pain.

- Dirty diapers

There are babies who can behave normal even with a wet diaper all day long while there are others who take the home down with their cries when their diaper is wet for just a while. Well, know your baby type and bless your soul if she comes in the latter category.

However, parenting is made easier nowadays as you don't have to sniff test to check if a diaper needs to be changed. There are color changeable diapers in the market these days which changes color when it's wet so you don't have to undress your child to check if the diaper is dirty.

So these are some of the reasons your baby must be crying. Now that you know, it will become easier for you to identify their worrisome gesture before it turns it into loud screaming cries. Also, if your child is not a loud crier, you should be extra careful as to what is bothering them when they whimper.

Babies often are fussy and they cry if anything is particularly stressful for them. And this is a very natural reaction because babies know no other way of communicating with you when they are distressed. However, it is important to calm your baby down when she is frantic and is crying because otherwise she will get worked up and might even fall sick. Given below are a few ways to soothe your baby.

- Place your baby on a carrier and slowly rock her while making calming sounds. You can try shushing softly and repeatedly and your baby will slowly soft crying. This works because when rocked, a baby's heart rate slows down and her muscles relax and they are much calmer than before while the sounds that you make become a welcome distraction for your baby.

- Sometimes too much noise and too bright lights can cause distress, leading your baby to cry and wail. In such cases, switch off all lights or at least dim them and rock your baby in your arms. Do not talk loudly (you can make occasional shushing sounds), but just snuggle your baby. Overstimulation is rather stressful for babies so allow them some quiet and dark to calm down.

- Music too has the power to calm and steady the respiratory rate of a crying baby. Therefore, you can softly hum lullabies or play different kinds of music to soothe your baby. While this helps your baby focus on the tunes rather than on crying, make sure that the music is not too loud and that it is familiar, because anything sudden or unfamiliar might just create the opposite effect and make your baby even more stressed and nervous.

- Distractions help a lot in soothing a crying baby, especially when it comes in the form of a change in scenery. Take your baby out for a walk in her stroller or carry her around the house. This will engage your baby's attention and soon your baby will stop crying.

- Many times babies cry for a very specific reason like they might be hungry or sleepy or maybe they are feeling too hot or too cold. Look out of any signs your baby might give to identify exactly what is causing your baby to cry. If you see that your baby is licking lips or sucking fingers or toes then it means he/ she is hungry or if your baby is yawning then that's a telltale sign that she needs to sleep now. So to avoid this, keep track of your baby's sleeping and feeding patterns and if your baby does start crying for any of these reasons then attend immediately and you can nurse your baby or gently lie her down on the bed and slowly soothe her, and this will allow your baby to drift off.

Before they learn to talk, babies use different signs and several sounds like coos and whimpers to communicate with you and to make you understand what they are feeling. But more often than not, they cry to indicate if something is distressing.

However, crying can be of different types and a baby will use different cries to tell you different things. The points below explain what these cries are and what they mean.

- Crying when hungry

Hunger cries have a very distinct tone. They are usually low pitched and repetitive, following a certain rhythm. Usually, this particular type of crying is accompanied by some other signs like rooting (where the baby moves her head from side to side and tries to find the breast to nurse), sucking on fingers and smacking lips.

When your baby is crying in this manner, you need to immediately respond and nurse your baby because otherwise she will become too upset and might start taking in air while nursing which will lead to spitting and throwing up and that will be even more stressful.

- Crying when bored

Sometimes, your baby will play on her own and enjoy that but there will be times when your baby will want attention and during this time, she will initially coo and try to alert you. However, if you do not respond immediately, then the cooing will intensify and your baby will fuss and whimper before starting to cry indignantly.

When this happens, all you need to is pick up your baby and snuggle a little and then engage with her by playing, singing or gently rocking back and forth.

- Crying when ill

Babies do fall ill at times but you should always look out for any symptoms of fever, rashes or diarrhea. When sick, your baby will cry softly and the cries will sound nasal and low pitched because they are tired and they do not have the energy to cry loudly.

Even though a slight fever or stomach upset is quite common babies, it is important to check how long the illness is persisting and what your baby's response is. If your baby is crying frantically, then you should check with your pediatrician immediately.

- Crying when uncomfortable

Many things might act as triggers to make you uncomfortable and to let you know that she will usually start with a nasal cry that will slowly intensify from whine to continuous crying. This will happen when your baby is tired of playing and needs a nap, or when the diaper is wet or is too hot or too cold.

It might be difficult to understand what exactly is making your baby cry but be sure to check if the diaper is clean, or look for signs that tell you she is sleepy (yawning, rubbing eyes) because babies will need a lot of sleep throughout the day and lack of it can make them fussy.

The only thing better than giving birth to your baby is seeing her laugh. Her first laugh is going to make a home in your heart and it will stay there forever.

While it is not easier for new-born kids to flex all those muscles and push laughter out because of weak body and under-developed muscle and jawline. It generally takes 3 to 4 months for a new-born to start laughing. You can always see your kid smile from the 1st or 2nd week after birth but a full-fledged will make you wait for 3-4 months.

While the first laughter of your new-born is worth the wait, you can take up some measures to help your kid push laughter out. A lot of kids simply fail to laugh even after 3 to 5 months because they do not know how to laugh, but if you help them exercise laughter, they will laugh and they will own very exquisite laughter.

Some of the common ways to make your baby laugh are:

- Start with funny sounds

Well! Laughter is nothing more than an expression of joy. Let your new-born experience some joy and they will laugh. Spend time with your kid making some funny noises and sound. Make efficient use of expressions to make those sounds appear real and authentic. The moment your newborn feels joyed, he or she will try to laugh by flexing muscles and jawline. Keep up with the momentum and a day will come when you will be able to see your newborn laugh like never before.

Newborns have always been slow with laughter and other expressions simply because of lack of exposure. Introduce them to new sounds, imitate a unique laughing style for them and see how they reciprocate.

- Eskimo kisses

Touch is perhaps the best way of building bonds with newborns. With the help of Eskimo Kisses, you can make your newborn laugh, giggle and experience joy. Eskimo kisses are basically bonding procedures where you tickle your newborn's face with your nose. Take your nose closer to their face and rub it gently to hear a giggle. Your kid is not going to laugh the very first time you do it, you will have to continue with the procedure for a 100 times before you hear them laugh for the first time.

- Peek-a-boo

This technique comes from time immemorial, people have been relying on this technique for ages. This has helped more kids laugh than any other technique. All you need to do is cover your face with something and say "Peek" and then scream "Boo" while revealing your face. Studies have shown that this technique urges the emotions inside kids making them feel happy and joyous.

- Photos of laughing baby

As mentioned earlier, to evoke laughter in your new-born, you will first have to introduce them to laughter. Put up a few posters of laughing baby and allow your kid to look at it for a few times in the day. The more they see a laughing baby, the more they will try to create a similar expression. By putting a poster of a laughing baby, you are allowing them to copy the expression and laugh in real life.

- Get your pets involved

If you have pets like cats or dogs at home, then it is now time for you to involve them to make your baby laugh. It is scientifically proven that animals generate a unique joy in kids making them smile and laugh. If your kid is strong enough to flex muscles, produce sound then he or she will laugh otherwise a smile is all that they will produce. Let your dog play with your kid, allow your newborn to touch the soft skin of your dog or cat, these touches will invoke emotions and joy.

- Let them bond with other kids

If a simple picture of a laughing baby can make your newborn laugh, think what a full-fledged baby can do? Get help from your friends or cousins, ask them to come over to your place with their kids. Allow your kid and their kid to spend some time together, let them play, let them do a lot of other things together. You will see with every passing second, your kid will become more and more open and joyous.

Making your baby's food on your own is actually a very easy process, especially because it does not involve many ingredients or any fancy, complicated steps. Also, making baby food at home allows you to decide what ingredients you will use ensuring that every meal is a hundred percent healthy. Given below are a few easy recipes that you can use to create a meal that is tasty and wholesome.

- Fruit Purees

Start by using one single fruit like an apple (peeled and washed) and puree it. Make sure to strain it so that your baby can swallow it easily. Once your baby is used to single fruit purees, start combining different fruits like bananas, berries, peaches to create smooth purees that are full of flavor. In these fresh fruit purees, you do not need to use salt and sugar if the fruit is sweet enough.

- Steamed Vegetables

This is an easy way to get your baby to eat vegetables. All you need to do is steam assorted vegetables like beans, spinach, broccoli, cauliflower florets and carrots (after peeling, and cleaning them thoroughly) with a bit of salt to taste. Now you can use the steamed vegetables to create a puree or simply mash them a bit and feed your baby.

- Meat Stew

Cut the meat (you can use beef chuck) into small pieces and toss it in all-purpose flour before adding it in a cooker with tomatoes, potatoes, peas, and carrots. Add salt to taste and cook on high heat till the meat is tender. Now place the contents of the cooker in a blender and create a puree of proper consistency.

- Lentils and Spinach

Lentils, especially red lentil is rich in protein and is very good for your baby. To create a lentil and spinach soup, boil the lentil with a bit of salt and add the spinach to give a creamy texture. You can also use a vegetable or a chicken broth to dilute the soup but make sure that your baby still finds it easy to digest.

- Poached Fish and Meat

Once you decide to feed fish and different types of meat to your baby, it is important to prepare the dish in a way that it becomes easily digestible and to do so, poaching is one of the best methods. When meat, fish or poultry is poached, the liquid retained keeps it soft and moist and you can now mash it together before feeding your baby.

- Slow Cooked Carrots and Apricots

This is a combination of sweet and savory and it allows you to combine fruit and vegetable together. Add diced carrots and apricots in a 4 to 6-quart slow cooker and cook on low heat, until the carrots are really soft and tender. Then, mash the carrots and apricots together and add a hint of nutmeg (optional and to taste) and stir before straining it to make it smooth.

Perhaps one thing which might leave you confused is if your baby is hungry yet or not.

Well, here are a few signs you should look for:

- Your baby has just woken up or is already awake and alert.

When your baby wakes up, she is going to be hungry, especially if it has been quite some time since the last meal. Also, if your baby has been awake for some time already and you find that she is unusually alert, it means that it's time to feed because your baby might feel a little tired or even a little stressed and hungry.

- Your baby is turning towards your breast while you hold her

For mothers who breastfeed their babies, this is a common sign that the baby is hungry. Your baby will constantly try to find a position for you to nurse and while you snuggle her, she might turn towards your breast or even try to pull at your clothes and lie back on your lap.

When infants who are breastfed do these things, this is a sure sign of the fact that they now need to be fed. This is also known as rooting where your baby will move her head from side to side, trying to find a nipple.

- Your baby is making faces and cooing and whimpering constantly.

Babies often start making faces or they make small sounds and sigh when something is particularly stressful for them and not always is it because they are hungry. But feeding your baby will help her stay calm and if it has been a while since you last fed, then it might be the right time to do so again.

- Your baby is unusually restless.

Babies become very fussy and restless when they are hungry. They might start hitting you on the arm repeatedly and sometimes, babies will start crying for no apparent reason. It might take you a while to figure out why your baby is crying or fussing, but most of the time, the reason is that your baby is hungry.

Due to hunger, babies will start fidgeting or squirming and even crying because that is the most common release, especially when something causes distresses and to calm them down, this is a good time to breastfeed or give a bottle fitted with a nipple to latch on.

- Your baby is licking lips or sucking on her lips, tongue or toes and fingers.

Infants are obviously not able to express hunger clearly and at a stage when they are hungry but not stressed because of it, they might give more subtle signs by licking their lips or constantly sucking their finger and toes or sometimes even toys and clothes or anything else they might get their hands on.

However, while playing babies will smack their lips or suck on something and this does not necessarily mean that they are hungry but it is important to keep track of mealtimes so that you know when your baby might give signs that he/ she is hungry.

New mothers often cannot choose between breastfeeding and bottle feeding their babies. While some mothers continue to breastfeed their babies, other mothers might not be able to do for several reasons like certain medical conditions, stress, lifestyle or even if they are working mothers with hectic schedules. In such instances, mothers choose to bottle feed their babies and in these cases, baby formula is actually quite a healthy and safe alternative.

Breastfeeding

Experts believe that breastfeeding should begin within one hour of the infant's life and can continue for as long as the infant wants it or as long as the mother is able to nurse her baby.

During the initial weeks, the baby will nurse up to ten or twelve times a day for almost fifteen minutes and once they grow older, they will not nurse so frequently. Regular breastfeeding decreases the risk of respiratory infections, bacterial meningitis, ulcerative colitis, and even sudden infant death syndrome.

Breastfeeding is also usually recommended because breast milk has several properties that are of great benefits, like:

- It contains polyunsaturated, long chain fatty acids that boost neural development and improve eyesight.
- It has colostrum which is produced during the first few days and has a laxative effect which prevents jaundice by secreting more bilirubin.
- It has the perfect amount of proteins, fat, water and sugar that is needed for the baby to grow strong.

Bottle Feeding

When mothers choose to bottle feed their babies, it does not mean that the babies will miss out on essential nutrients and not grow up fast enough or not be healthy enough. It is important to find the correct formula which will suit the baby and then bottle feeding can be done with ease.

The formula used should have the right vitamins, minerals, and other components and this should not be very difficult because the baby formula that is available usually tries to replicate the components of breast milk and recreate the optimum combination of protein, fat, sugar, and vitamins and minerals. Some formulas also have a supplement base which might be of extra benefit to the baby.

The main reasons why a mother should bottle feed her baby are as follows:

- It is a very convenient process and can be done by either parent without any hassle.
- A mother can attend to other tasks while bottle feeding her baby and this allows her to multitask.
- Mothers do not have to worry about following strict diets when they decide to bottle feed their babies.

Which Is More Appropriate?

While most doctors will recommend breastfeeding, it is actually up to the mothers as to what they feel most comfortable with. New mothers can choose to bottle feed their babies after the first few days of breastfeeding and to ease the process they can even pump out their breast milk and store it in a bottle which can be used before trying a formula.

Circumcision in males involves the removal of the foreskin from the penis. In circumcision, the foreskin is usually opened to remove the adhesions and then the foreskin is separated. In some procedures, once the foreskin is removed from the glans, a circumcision device is placed to cut the foreskin off. The usage of a circumcision device allows one to avoid general anesthesia and many decide to go for local anesthesia.

The practice of circumcision usually is a ritual in several religions or is seen as a cultural practice and is mostly an elective surgery that parents decide to have performed upon their children. However, sometimes, it is also done for medical conditions like chronic urinary tract infections, phimosis or balanoposthitis.

Male circumcision is also said to reduce the risk of HIV infection and even the cancer-causing human papillomavirus and it also sometimes protects from several sexually transmitted diseases.

In infants or toddlers, parents usually decide to have them circumcised due to religious practices and given below are some points that should always be kept in mind after the circumcision is done.

- The lubricant gauze which is used as dressing should not be removed before twenty-four hours. The gauze is a protective dressing and it helps the area to heal faster, preventing any chance of immediate infection.
- In infants, after changing a messy diaper, clean the penis using warm water and baby soap. Make sure to use a soft washcloth or baby wipes.
- For a few weeks after the surgery, it is recommended that you only provide sponge baths to your baby boy and avoid making her completely wet. Wait till the incision has completely healed before you start giving full baths.

- Every time you bathe your infant or change his diaper, make sure to apply some ointment (one that is recommended by the doctor) or petroleum jelly on the end of the penis. It is not necessary to keep the penis covered with a bandage at all times but you can also apply petroleum jelly or antibiotic ointment on the incision and then place a bandage over it. But it is advisable that you first consult your doctor before doing this because once the dressing is off, you usually do not require another bandage for the healing process to continue.

- If your baby boy is experiencing some pain after circumcision, then you can consult the concerned doctor and then give acetaminophen which will provide relief. But make sure that it's just for slight, occasional pain and if the pain persists then immediately take your baby for a checkup.

- After circumcision, typically there is no bleeding, or swelling and redness. But if any of this happens, accompanied by a fever or if there is any yellowish fluid leaking from the incision that has not fully healed or if your baby is experiencing pain while urinating, then immediately take him to the nearest hospital because all this might be because of some infection or even if the surgery has not been done and dressed properly.

- Toddlers are sometimes quite active and especially if they are just learning to walk. Therefore strict supervision should be maintained at all times because your toddler might end up straining himself a bit too much and if this happens right after the surgery then there might be a considerable amount of pain followed by oozing or even bleeding at times.

- Often circumcision is not done at the infant stage, but later when the child grows a little older, usually when he is about eight to ten years old. Sometimes circumcision is also done in adolescent boys. In both cases, some essential tips must be known that involve taking care of themselves once the surgery is done and those are mentioned below.

- Preadolescent or adolescent boys are usually very active. But for two weeks after the surgery, they should avoid rough sports or restrict their activity to the bare minimum because being too active might lead to the incision splitting and can cause oozing, accompanied by pain.

- After the surgery, the doctor will wrap a bandage around, but it should be removed a day after. Removing the bandage becomes easier after sitting under the shower for about ten minutes and slowly unwrapping the entire dressing. After removing the bandage, allow the water to dry before applying Vaseline or some ointment like bacitracin around the incision. This should be done several times a day as it prevents the incision on the penis from sticking to clothes which might cause some friction leading to an uncomfortable feeling.

- Tight shorts or pants should not be worn before the sutures are completely healed as the cloth might rub against the incision leading to itching or oozing.

- The incision might ooze and there might be some bruising around it. But this is a part of the healing process after circumcision and there is usually no cause for being alarmed. The fluid oozing out can be cleaned using a tissue, but care should be taken that it is done gently. If the oozing continues for a long time or is followed be bleeding, then the concerned doctor should be immediately consulted.

For a few days following circumcision, there might be some pain and that is normal. It can be relieved by taking medicines like Tylenol or if necessary then a combination of Tylenol with codeine. But it is important to keep in mind that these pain relief drugs should be taken only after consulting a doctor and the prescription should be followed strictly when it comes to the dosage.

While taking care after the circumcision is important, it is also equally important to visit the doctor for regular check-ups, till the incision heals completely. This way, it can be known if the healing process is happening the way it should and also if there is any extra precaution that needs to be taken.

Toddlers are usually picky eaters and during this stage, babies do fuss at mealtimes but in case of newborns, feeding is not a hassle but they need to be fed all the time and thus, mothers need to constantly monitor their schedules. However, sometimes, newborns can be fussy too and they might not want to nurse.

After feeding your baby, burping will help your baby to expel the air which has been taken in while feeding. If too much air is swallowed then it might make her spit up or which is bound to make your baby uncomfortable.

Feeding

Given below are a few tricks that you can use to feed your baby if she is fussing.

- Do not feed anything other than breast milk or baby formula to your new-born. While breast milk is ideal, baby formulas also have a good balance of supplements, proteins, vitamins, sugar and fat which is sufficient for your baby to grow healthy.
- Stay alert about your baby's feeding schedules. While newborns need to be nursed eight to ten times a day, once they grow older, they will not feed so many times and you need to allow them to figure out when they want to eat. So, when they are a little older, with flexible mealtimes, present a range of options and your toddler might actually eat several portions without fussing.
- Now once your baby is a little older, you will want to try some other foods like steamed vegetables and fruits. To do this, place small pieces on the feeding tray and allow them to touch and see the food. Some babies might automatically place it in their mouths, while others take a little time.

Burping

Follow the tricks given below to easily burp your baby.

- Cup your hand and gently pat your baby on the back while holding her.
- Sometimes your baby might spit up or have a wet burp and to avoid a mess, keep a towel on your shoulder which can be used to wipe your baby's chin and mouth.
- Try different positions for burping. If holding your baby, while standing is not doing the trick, then holding up your baby on your lap, gently gripping her chin, and slowly pat on the back. You can also lay your baby on her belly and then pat.

Diapering

Babies, especially during the first few weeks, need about eight to ten diapers throughout the day. Later, if a baby has not been potty trained or has the tendency of bedwetting, then he/ she will require diapers but possibly not too many each day. Diapers need to be changed as frequently as required to prevent any skin problems that may arise due to wearing a messy diaper for a long time.

New parents might not be at ease with changing diapers and it might take them a while to figure out what is the best way to change a diaper. However, following the basics given below, parents or caregivers will be able to keep things organized and be able to change the baby's diaper quite easily.

- Take out the diaper from its packaging (if it is a disposable diaper) and lay it out. If you are using cloth diapers, you have the fasteners ready.
- Fill a container with warm water and dip cotton balls in it. Cotton balls are recommended by pediatricians, especially if the baby has sensitive skin. Also, keep diaper wipes ready or you can also use a clean, soft washcloth.
- Lay out a changing pad over which you can place your baby while changing the diaper or even for laying out the cloth diaper.
- Always keep some petroleum jelly or diaper ointment. Massaging gently will prevent any skin rashes.
- The following steps on how to change a diaper, once you have all the supplies arranged and within reach, will make the process much easier than it appears to be.
- Place your baby on the changing pad or the changing table and always place a hand on your baby or use safety straps because babies wiggle around a lot.

- Lift your baby's legs out and gently slide the dirty diaper out.
- Use cotton balls dipped in warm water or a wet washcloth to gently clean your baby. Wipe from front to back, especially for baby girls, because you do not want to spread bacteria which might result in urinary tract infection. Lift your baby's legs and clean the underside and buttocks thoroughly and always wipe the creases in the thighs.

If you are using a disposable diaper then make sure that the adhesive tabs of the diaper approximately reach up to the level of the belly button and they go in the back. For a baby boy, make sure that the new diaper is placed over his penis because if that is not done, then they might urinate out of the top of the diaper. Similarly, if you are using a cloth diaper, then make sure to lay it out flat and then fold it over, using fasteners or Velcro straps to keep it in place.

Once you close the adhesive tabs or the straps, make sure that the diaper has been fitted properly and to do this, you can slip in two fingers between the diaper and your baby's tummy. It's important to keep in mind that the diaper should be snug but not too tight.

Swaddling

The practice of swaddling a baby is actually quite old and it involves wrapping your baby in a blanket. Now the idea of swaddling is not to restrict your baby, but rather because new-borns actually feel secured and content when they are swaddled. Some experts also believe that swaddling has some psychological as well as medical benefits and often it helps babies to fall asleep easily. Now while swaddled, a sleeping baby will always lie horizontally, facing upwards and this reduces the risk of the sudden infant death syndrome.

While swaddling might look easy because it's simply wrapping your baby in a few clothes and blankets, it is important to keep the following points or the basics of swaddling in mind.

- The blanket used should be of a proper size. You will not be able to wrap a small blanket and a large one will be too loose and your baby can easily remove it by kicking it off.

- Make sure that the cloth or blanket that you are using is soft but light because you do not want to create any more thermal insulation than what is required.

- You can use a specialized blanket that is meant only for swaddling. These blankets are usually of different shapes (triangular or in T or Y shape) and they come with Velcro straps.

- A traditional fabric blanket can also be used. These are larger and square and they can be used to swaddle your baby snugly.

- It is important to keep in mind that swaddling should either be done from birth or not at all. Do not suddenly start swaddling your baby after a couple of months because that might make your baby uncomfortable.

- Swaddling should be done carefully so that the fit is exactly how it is supposed and not too tight or too loose. If the fit is too tight then the baby might develop hip dysplasia, which happens if he/ she cannot move his/ her legs, allowing no room for flexibility and hip development. To prevent any such risks, follow the steps given below to ensure that your baby is swaddled properly.

- If you are using a traditional, square blanket, then lay it out in a diamond shape and place your baby on it. Make sure that your baby's back is right at the center of the fabric and the shoulders are below the fold.

- Take your baby's right arm and place it beside the body. Pull the same side of the blanket across the arm and over the chest.

- Now, gently fold the bottom of the blanket over the feet and slip in the top of the fabric.

- Take the left arm and wrap the remaining part of the blanket over the chest and tuck it around the back, which will completely secure the swaddle.

55

Easy Games You Can Play With Your Baby!

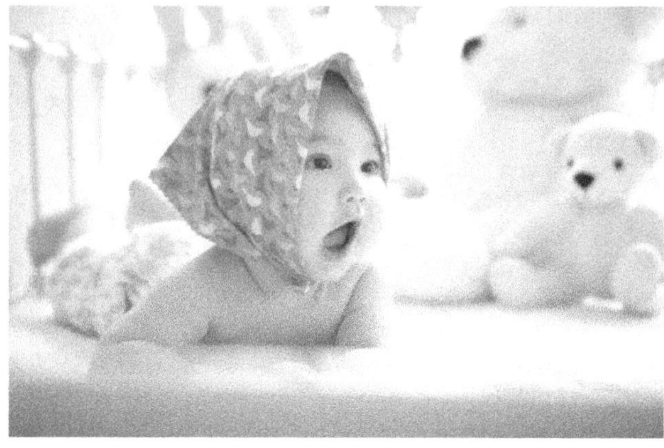

Many parents are confused about what kind of games they can play with their kids to aid in the growth of their kids in the very early years of their lives. It is very important to choose the right kinds of games for your kids.

Researchers say that it is never too early to play games with your kids to help them develop their communication, sensory movements, feeding and motor reflexes. These games may vary on the basis of the kid's age and the number of years of the kid's life. Some of the simplest games and activities can be listed as below and each one of them is specific for certain age groups of babies.

Motor activities

For kids within the age range of 0-3 months, it is very important to have a bond with the mother. Skin touch with the mother is very important at these stages to propel the growth of the baby. For mothers, it can be very challenging at times. Some of the easy activities a mother can have with the newborn may include:

- Place the newborn on the tummy and let him or her play on its own for a few times every day for a few minutes at a time.
- Place the baby on your tummy face down so that you face each other and let her play for a while. This would help the baby interact with you in sign languages while you are at it.
- Rock and sway the baby and hold them close to your body while you do it.
- Encourage the baby to twist and turn in the bed. You can change the direction in which the baby sleeps so that they change the position themselves while attaining their regular sleeping posture.
- Hold the hands of the baby and clap them while you sing a song or hum a tune.

Sensory Activities

Sensory activities are very important for a newborn as it would help the kid to perceive the surrounding in a better form and be able to form relationships with people around as well as objects. The senses of touch, feel, sound and the like can be build up using these activities. Some of the sensory activities may include:

Hanging a colorful mobile with different objects above the baby's crib which will provide certain visual stimulation for the kid. It is good if the baby is intrigued by the movement of the mobile and even better if it tries to reach it. It helps to give an idea about distance and touch to the kid.

- Tickling the baby and making her laugh might also be a good and fun activity to increase the sensory reflexes of the baby.
- Skin to skin contact with the baby might also be a very effective activity for increasing the bond between the caregiver or the parent and the baby.
- Smile at the baby, touch the forehead, hold the hand and feet see the reaction of the baby, and play with voices to make the baby laugh and giggle.
- Play songs or sing them to the baby, this might help the baby to develop listening skills. Repeat songs on days to see if the baby shows any signs of recognizing the verses of the tune.
- Move the baby around and play with them in different postures to enable the movement of the baby.
- Play the mirror game with the baby. Hang a mirror on the wall. Keep touching the image of the baby on the mirror and calling out his name. Eventually the baby with start figuring out who the kid is in the mirror.
- To spread positivity for the baby flip to family albums, randomly point to happy faces of people, you could even go a step further and ask who each of them are. However, make sure to keep it short and simple.

Communication Games

Communication activities play a vital role in the first year of a baby's life. It is important to make the right gesture and teach the correct forms of communication to the baby. There are a few things which you could do for the same. They are:

- Being a caregiver or a parent, you should give some proper face to face time for the baby.

- You can shake and dance with the baby on your lap while you sing a song. This might help the baby to understand your movements and move along.
- Use somewhat a high pitched voice or sing-song voice while speaking to the baby. It makes it easier for the baby to follow, perceive and remember what you are doing and trying to say and also holds on to the attention of the baby.
- Describing the actions while you feed, bathe or dress the baby will also help you to understand what the baby's interests are and make them understand the surrounding activities better.
- Take a doll and start by pointing at different body parts of the doll and name them out aloud for the baby.

<u>Feeding Activities</u>

Feeding is a very important time for a baby and you can make the best use of it to allow the baby to learn and grow.

You can use the sense of smell to see what the baby prefers. For this, you can bring certain flowers, perfumes and spices one at a time in front of the baby's nose and see how they perceive each smell and which one they tend to prefer.

There are similar games for 4-6 month olds. Some of which are described below.

Motor activities

- Place the baby on his or her tummy on a blanket and move the blanket around in the house.
- Allow the baby to play with toys with the hand and mouth but make sure that the toys are large enough to prevent choking for the baby.
- Allow the baby to roll on his or her tummy and back. Rolling is one of the very first signs of strengthening the back and the muscles which would eventually help the baby stand up and walk.
- Place different toys around the baby so that they try to roll over and grab them as and when they try to collect them.

Sensory Activities

- The sensory activities of kids within this age group might involve a little more serious stuff. You can make use of various kinds of fabric such as wool, velvet and the like to make sure that the baby gets a full on experience of the feel of each one of them and spot the difference.
- Take the baby up and down while you play with her so that the baby can form an idea about movement and balance at the same time.
- Showing the baby how to drop bounce and throw a ball will help her to get an idea about speed and distance.
- You can make use of different textured and different colored balls to play with the kid as well.

<u>Communication Games</u>

- Peek-a-boo is a fun game that you can play with your baby.
- Reading with the baby or simply describing things on the go might also help in the communication developmental process of the baby.
- The baby babbles and coos, encourage a two-way conversation for the baby. Try to communicate with the baby as he or she tries to communicate with you.
- Toys that make sound are a good choice at this age for the baby.

Motor Games

- Place different toys around the baby where they need to move around to reach and grab them at a time.
- Pushups for the baby by lowering and raising rattles are also good motor activity.
- When the baby is holding two toys in two hands, offer them a third and see how the baby thinks for themselves and figures out how to hold the third toy without letting go of the two that are already in hand.
- Use an empty bucket and teach your kid to throw all toys in it. This not only does keep the house clean but also nurtures good habits in the kid.
- Use squeeze toys and other household items to make different noises for the baby.

Sensory Games

- Shadow puppets are a very good way to entertain and teach the baby
- Making the baby giggle by touching the different parts of the body can also be fun and might improve the sensory reflexes of the baby at this stage.
- Walk with the baby
- Let the baby explore the environment freely and keep a close eye on them
- Make use of toys of various colors, shapes, and sizes to see if the baby recognizes them.
- Let the baby explore the items within its reach but stay close to ensure that they do not choke on any small item.
- Incorporate different textures. Make use of the different soaps, creams, and sponges to give the baby a proper idea about textures.
- Skin-to-skin touch is also very important at this stage.

Communication Games

- Draw a baby's face and point out the different parts in it.
- Play with a toy phone and pretend to have a serious conversation on that call and then hand over the phone to the baby and see how he or she react.
- Read short stories to and with the baby
- Start teaching hand movements and gestures to the baby while talking and making use of different words
- Play music for the baby throughout the day.
- Face time is very important at this stage of life
- Pointing out objects while you talk to the baby is very important.

Feeding activities

- Introduce pureed food to the baby's diet but make sure to avoid cow's milk, honey, salt and any kinds of artificial sweeteners.
- Introduction of certain new items to the baby's diet and see what the reaction is.
- Changing the texture of the food is a good idea in case the baby refuses to take certain food.
- A healthy diet for the baby is very essential at this stage.

Motor games

- Let the baby have stack toys and blocks and ask them to explain each toy as they pick them. This is a good exercise to ensure the describing ability of the baby.
- Allow the baby to crawl over your while you lie down on the floor.
- New hand gestures should be done in front of the baby such as clapping, blowing kisses and the like
- Allow the baby to play with large objects, a pillow could be one of them,
- Encourage the baby to stand up and walk.
- Sway and dance with the baby along with the music.
- Slow rocking movements are encouraged as well.

Sensory games

- Introduction to different textures and textiles in terms of food and clothing is a fun way to improve the sensory reflexes of the baby.
- Keep the baby away from smoke and harsh chemicals at all times
- Skin-to-skin contact is again a very useful aspect which plays a huge role in the developmental process of the baby.

Communication Games

- Having a look at the baby's reflection is a very thoughtful way of teaching the baby as to how it works
- Take away the baby's attention at interesting objects and try to name or point at the object. This way one would be able to understand the interest of the baby and thus act accordingly.
- Ask the baby to say 'Hello' when they meet new people.

- The response should always be given to the baby's babbling and cooing
- The questioning ability of the baby should be encouraged at all time. Only if they question and are able to reason out they will be able to grow in life as a person.

<u>Feeding skills</u>

- Offer the baby a variety of food to choose from.
- Any kind of unhealthy and inappropriate food should be kept out of the kid's diet.

Issues That Babies Often Face

Jaundice

Jaundice is one of the most common ailments in infants. In the contemporary world, the advancement of the medical domain has made it easier for everyone to identify and get rid of diseases which were difficult in older days, jaundice was one of the most prominent causes of death. Infant jaundice occurs due to the presence of Bilirubin, a yellow pigment in excess. The production of Bilirubin increases as more and more red blood cells break down.

Basically, the crippled growth of liver in infants promotes the growth of Bilirubin, thus leading to jaundice more often than in adults

The good thing about infant jaundice is that it cures on its own as soon as the liver starts to develop. When the infant starts to consume staple food, the bilirubin is then passed through the liver and intestine along with other food materials, making it easier for the body to recover from jaundice. It takes a maximum of 2 to 3 weeks for Bilirubin to pass out of the infant's body, if the problem persists for more than 3 weeks, jaundice may be due to other reasons and it is suggested to get in touch with a doctor.

Too much production of Bilirubin in an infant can lead to lethal problems like deafness, damages to brain and cerebral palsy. It is advised to be frequent with checks if your baby is experiencing high production of Bilirubin. In varied countries, it is now becoming a norm to check babies for overproduction of bilirubin before releasing them from the hospitals.

What Causes New-Born Jaundice?

- Infection is perhaps the main cause of infant jaundice

Delivering a baby in a hospital that doesn't follow requisite measures of cleanliness and sanitization will have diverse effects on the health of your newborn baby. Hospitals are generally loaded with infectious bacteria and viruses and lack of cleanliness triggers their propagation, thus making it tough for the newborn kids to keep away from harmful diseases.

Infection also occurs when the newborn kid is allowed to meet with a lot of people and hospital staff. Everyone that gets close to the newborn must be provided with sanitizer to clean their hands before touching the baby. Since babies tend to lick everything, the chances of infection spreading are always highest.

- Premature babies

The risk of acquiring infant jaundice is highest in premature babies because the liver is not fully grown and requires additional time for optimal growth. The delay in growth of the liver makes it tough for the body to throw Bilirubin out of the body. Any baby that is delivered under 37 weeks of Gestion will face problems like infant jaundice more often. A baby that has spent its due period in the womb is ready to face the attacks of viruses in the real world.

- Babies experiencing lack of breast milk

A lot of babies acquire infant jaundice either because they are not provided with sumptuous breast milk or they are unable to digest it. Premature babies generally face issues with breast milk digestion and require additional supplement in place of breast milk.

- When the baby's blood type is not compatible with mothers

If all the varied causes of infant jaundice are studied, you will realize all of them are connected to each other. The risk of infant jaundice increases when the blood group of mothers is different or not compatible with the blood of the baby.

Any blood group mismatch or non-compatibility will increase the risk of infant jaundice. In such cases, keeping a check on the production of Bilirubin is perhaps the most important step. One needs to ensure that the requisite measures like medication or change in the supplement is acquired to reduce the production of Bilirubin.

Some of the other common causes of infant jaundice are:

- Internal bleeding due to bruises or scratches during delivery of the baby
- Undeveloped liver, weak liver or less capability of digestion
- Any kind of infection either due to mother's health or due to instruments used for assisting delivery
- Lack of proper production of a particular enzyme in the infant
- Any kind of abnormality in the red blood cells leading to more production of Bilirubin

What Are The Most Common Symptoms of Infant Jaundice?

The most common symptom of infant jaundice is yellowing of skin and eyes. Infant jaundice generally triggers after 2 days of delivery reaching to its peak on 7th or 8th day after delivery. One can easily spot it from the face because it is from where it starts and then spreads across the body.

Yellowing of a body is highly visible on face specially in the eyes, one look at those little eyes turning yellow and the doctor will confirm whether the baby is suffering from infant jaundice or not.

It is highly recommended to keep an eye and look for any such symptoms because infant jaundice can be a tough task to deal with when caught in the later stage.

We have already discussed the lack of breast milk production and consumption as the root causes of infant jaundice but we also need to understand a few more things:

- Eating habits of the mother effects the overall health of the baby

It is okay to say that infant jaundice can occur due to bad eating habits of the pregnant mother. Yes! A pregnant woman that constantly feeds on junk food will have less breast milk being produced in her body leading to a lack of nutrients to the newborn kid, which will stop the development of liver leading to accumulation of Bilirubin in the kid's body.

One needs to understand the varied nuances and always avoid consuming a lot of unhealthy food when they are due.

- Obstructive jaundice caused by Hernia

It is now a common cause of infant jaundice. With eating problems and infections being the leading cause of jaundice, the hernia is growing in the popularity list. A lot of cases of infant jaundice have popped up where hernia played a crucial role in the development of the disease.

Congenital diaphragmatic hernia is the reason a lot of kids acquire jaundice as soon as they are born. One of the best ways of restricting the occurrence of infant jaundice due to congenital diaphragmatic hernia is proper ultrasound verification of the baby after birth. It is important to carry out one such ultrasound under the 2 days of delivery to ensure any such probability of occurrence of infant jaundice is discovered and restricted.

Congenital diaphragmatic hernia leading to infant jaundice is not a common phenomenon but in the contemporary world where pregnant mothers are fed with food that is contaminated and carries a lot of fertilizers nothing can be said.

Child's Traits

Traits are inborn and usually remain the same throughout life. However, a bad trait can be mended with ease and patience at an early age easily. It is for the parents how they find the good in their child despite the child's traits and work towards managing and dealing with them in the right manner.

Parenting is not as easy as it seems as it is more of intellectual activity. Here are some of the activities that will help you to understand your child's traits well.

- Activity

Activity is a child's primary trait that let us know the degree of physical motion a child has. If a child is enthusiastic the whole day and keep playing without feeling sleepy, he is high on activity. Such kids can't sit at one place and are restless.

As a parent, you would know even changing a diaper can be big trouble with such kids as they can't stay still for even a minute. However, such kids are usually good at sports.

On the other hand, kids with low activity are slow movers as they prefer to stay at the same place for hours. They are more into mind activities rather than physical activities. As a parent, you should never label your kid as lazy rather teach him the importance of moving around and make him do some activities.

- Regularity

Does your child wake up at the same time every day, does he follow the same schedule of activities during the day? Is he following the same routine of eating, sleeping, and other living activities at the same time or are they done whenever he feels like arbitrarily and unpredictably?

Regularity refers to following a disciplined pattern when it comes to behavioral activities and predicting these biological patterns in your children. It is an important trait to know your child pattern. You can predict your child's regularity by following their biological functions like appetite, sleep, bowel movements, tiredness, etc.

A child with low regularity is hard to predict and it can't be known when they would be hungry, sleepy or otherwise. However, such children turn out to be flexible which in turn help them while travelling or switching jobs.

On the other hand, a child with high regularity is more into following a set pattern every day with no deviation.

- Initial approach

This trait is concerned with your child being an introvert or extrovert. It refers to your child's initial instinct towards experiencing something or meeting someone new, towards new places, ideas, etc. Is your child withdrawing or shying away when meeting new people or does he get mixed up and friendly with anyone too easily?

Children who are introvert are more cautious, careful and think twice before acting which is regarded as a good trait, however they are considered to be slow to adapt and are inflexible to changes. The children who fall in the latter category are children with the initial approach. They are outgoing, tend to be more social and like to embrace new things in life. But they are fast decision makers as well, and act impulsively and jump into conclusions without paying heed.

Know the category in which your child falls and try to condition them accordingly. If your child is an introvert, do not expect them to be an extrovert. Accept them as they are! If your child is quick-to-approach, help him in being more cautious, likewise if your child is slow to warm, help him in being comfortable and make him understand what all can happen when he is outing.

- Adaptability

Adaptability trait lets you know if your child is flexible to changes or not after their initial approach. Some children are very adaptable and accept things as they are. They don't fuss about any change in their routine. Such children in their teens are more into standing affirm whatever life throws at them. They have high adaptability and transition does not bother them.

On the other hand, some children have low adaptability and they are not good with the transition. They have a hard time when things don't go as per their routine. Such children are not quick to adapt to changes and are close to throwing more tantrums.

Thus, this character trait is closely related to the approach and withdrawal trait discussed above.

As a parent of low adaptability trait, you should warn them a little before any transition takes places as this will make it easier for them to accept the change as they would be informed beforehand.

- Sensitivity

Does your child cry and gets sad easily over trifle matters? Or they just cry enough to show how they are feeling? Does a cloth tag or a wet diaper annoy him a lot? Does she shut her ears with her hands when in a crowdy place? Or is she not bothered with whatever comes and goes around her stimuli and is always cheerful regardless?

In whatever category your child falls in, this is about how sensitive is your child emotionally and sensibly. Children with high sensitivity require careful parenting as they can be really temperamental and react more violently then they should. They are more dramatic. Whereas, a low sensitivity kid is easy to deal with as they don't react to their changing stimuli that strongly. They are cheerful and happy in every situation.

As a parent, you should not keep labelling your kid as oversensitive and do not point out to others that he/she cries easily. Instead use words which sound more positive like softhearted, tender, generous, discriminating, etc. also, if your child has low sensitivity, label him has easy going, accepting, flexible.

- Intensity

This character trait refers to the level of energy with which your child responds to news, ideas, and events taking place, positively or negatively.

Children with high intensity tend to respond to things too brightly or too arrogantly. When they are happy, they are extremely happy and when they are angry, they can bring the house down with their screams. However, this makes them better at showing their emotions than children with low intensity.

A child with low intensity is always calm and react to things with the same intensity. Such kids are not good at showing their emotions and can be gloomy when adult.

As a parent of high-intensity kid, you have to be patient with them. Remember not to be harsh at them at the same time when they are throwing tantrums. Let them calm down and then make them understand what is needed to be told.

Whereas, if you have a low-intensity kid, you have to be extra attentive on how they are feeling in each situation as they are not that expressive and respond mildly in every situation.

- Mood distractibility

Distractibility is an important trait which refers to the degree by which your kid gets deviated or lose attention when he is involved in an activity he isn't interested in. This usually happens while studying. Kids tend to be more prone to find distractions when they are made to study. This is when they allow the external stimuli to interfere which their current pattern of activity. The ease with which your child is able to shush this external stimulus, the low is your child's distractibility and vice-a-versa.

Low distractibility can be good as well as bad. It seems to be in parents favor when your child is made to study while it seems as bad enough when he needs to be distracted from an activity which is undesirable or counts as bad behavior.

Kids with high distractibility can also be more observant and keep due notice about what is happening around them. It is also easy to divert their mood when they are sad or upset.

Kids with low distractibility are more attentive, focused and have high concentrating power. They are not side tracked by external stimuli and are highly engrossed in whatever they do. However, it is difficult with them when they need to be warded off something they should not do.

- Persistence

It is the degree to which a child will be keen on accomplishing a task even at the time of facing obstacles or failure. Does he keep on trying and trying and is persistent to achieve success be it in solving a puzzle, opening a bottle cap, learning to ride a bicycle, etc.? If so, your kid is highly persistent.

Kids with high persistence do not give up easily and stick to it until it's done. Such kids make up ambitious teens and do not leave things half done. They don't lose hope even when it gets difficult.

Kids with low persistence are prone to give up when they start facing an obstacle. They like things to be smooth and when they start facing hurdles, they tend to give up. As a result, their mind isn't that open to new ideas and are always in need of other's help in finishing a task.

So, these were some of the child's trait that can help you to understand better. Remember, just be with them and help them be a better person.

Newborn's Behavior

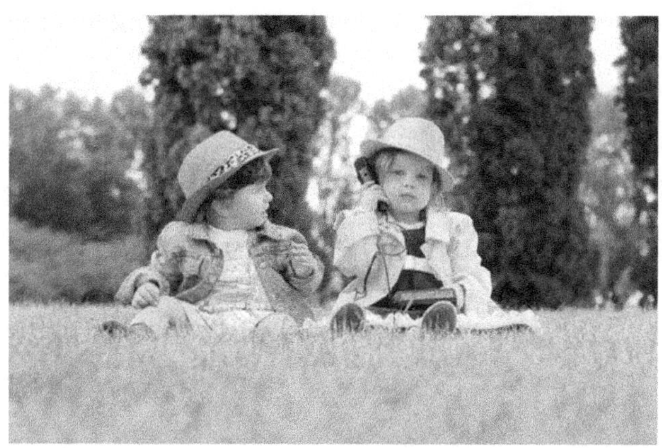

A lot of newbie parents tend to get scared on seeing their new-born behave erratically, what they do not understand is the fact that it is her first day on the planet and it is quite different from the inside of the womb.

While a woman's womb is designed to cater to requisite growth and stability, the atmosphere on earth is different even though it supports life. The temperature, lighting, and presence of other pigments in the atmosphere is a new kind of experience for the infant. While some adjust quickly to the atmosphere outside some take their time.

It is completely okay for your new-born to cry, shout, feel agitated, appear curious, and be highly active and sensitive too. You should keep calm and seek your doctor's opinion on everything instead of taking measures on your own. A lot of kids are generally born in hospitals where temperature and lighting is maintained keeping the newborns in mind whereas the few kids who are born through normal delivery at home face issues with temperature and lighting. Too much of light is a new experience for the infants because the inside of womb is completely dark and their eyes are not ready to handle a lot of light.

Well! The only time you need to worry about your kid's behavior is when she is a premature baby. Not only she requires extra medical attention but keeping an eye on her behavior is equally important too.

You must take requisite steps to see that she is comfortable and not experiencing varied kind of pain under extreme medical supervision. Since premature baby is kept under stimulated conditions to provide a growth similar to the womb, they might experience agitation and a little kind of weary pain. Doctors generally oversee any such circumstances but parents must keep an eye and report at the earliest to the doctors.

- Highly Active

A new-born kid that is ecstatic and highly active represents good health. It is proof that the kid is healthy and is prepared for the real world. A highly active kid also exhibits that she has received proper nutrition during the pregnancy period and is well groomed for handling the outer world. Doctors generally run checks for jaundice and other infections in kids who are little dull and irritated but with highly active kids, they are quite sure and relaxed.

- Very curious

Studies have proved that kids look forward to copying expressions and actions in order to bond faster with people around. During the initial days, your kid will put efforts in to copying everything you do or express, while it might be difficult for them to actually copy but they will remain curious about. Since a lot of people will be coming and greeting them, they will grow even more curious and may react to it differently.

Kids from around the world have shown the tendency of being curious because of being exposed to a completely new world.

- Persistent

This is one condition that varies from kids to kids, if your kid is persistent with high activeness, then it is a good thing for you but if your kid is irritated or keeps crying for a long time, it means he or she requires medical attention. It is very normal for a newborn to be highly active and sleepy for the rest of time. Any kid that feels irritated on a regular basis might be suffering from a medical condition and might require a doctor's attention and supervision.

A healthy kid will make use of her energy to showcase their anxiety, express their curiosity and also react to varied stimuli. Your actions will be reciprocated, your expressions will be imitated and your gestures will be reciprocated.

- Intense Irregular

New parents tend to get scared once their kid starts behaving differently. It is completely okay for your new-born to behave differently than the previous kids born in your family. Every kid is a new human with a new body grown in a different condition. The health of the mother during pregnancy has huge effects on kids' health and behavior. An unhealthy mother cannot give birth to a healthy kid and it is quite possible that a lot of diseases, infection, and allergies gets transferred to the newborn.

Intense and irregular behavior is a matter of concern, either the new-born is highly uncomfortable with the lighting, bed, temperature or is suffering from a medical condition. You might try to dim the lights, control the temperature or change the kid's posture to see if anything changes or simply request a doctor's attention. Going ahead with medical attention request is always a good move under all conditions.

- Quite and Content

Healthy kids who are responding well to expressions and breast =feeding will grow content and quite over the kids. It is a good sign for mother and new-born, a content kid will do a lot of activities and go back to sleep, unlike kids who are suffering from medical conditions. A quiet kid will express their hunger through crying and irritation and will become quite again once they are fed well.

The varied conditions are a result of the nutrients that the mother consumed during pregnancy, while too much of iron and calcium makes a baby highly active and jovial, other oxidized nutrients make them quiet and calm. It is also important to take medicines during pregnancy only after consulting with the doctor. A lot of medicines increase complications while delivery forcing C Section.

- Easily Frustrated

Not all kids even from the same mother are going to be quiet and calm because all of them are different and all of them are groomed according to the condition of womb while they were inside it. Any kid that has too much iron or calcium will turn out to be highly active while others might appear to be frustrating and irritating. Your kid requires medical attention and additional support if they are too much frustrated or seem to be agitated all the time.

An easily frustrated kid might be tired and requires extra comfort. You need to let your kid sleep for longer hours if they are getting easily frustrated. Stop too much interaction with new people, stop moving them around from one person to another in arms, and put them to rest in a comfortable position in a comfortable bed.

- Slow to adapt

There's not a lot that can be said about the kids who are slow to adapt because most of them are slow in the first few days and then pick up their pace in the second week. Kids have shown great activeness in first few days and then grew comfortable making doctors assume they have adapted to the situation while some kids take over a week or two to adjust to conditions around them.

A kid that is slow to adapt will cry, feel irritated and disturb their parents a little but they are completely normal and there's nothing to panic about it. Give your kid time to grow used to the outside world, new people, new stimulus and new conditions.

- Distractible

In middle terms, a kid who is easily distracted might be suffering from ADHD, which is a medical term for inattentiveness. Kids suffer from such issues all the time and there's nothing anything to worry about. Reporting it to doctor for medical attention is perhaps the only solution.

When kids are regularly breast feed and provided with the requisite comfort, they grow out of these illnesses and become healthy. They grow attentive over the time and responds to various people around them.

- Highly sensitive

Around 15 to 20 percent kids in the world are born with highly sensitive nervous system. This condition is nothing something hazardous or worrisome, it is simply a unique combination of health, medicines and nervous system. Presence of a few nutrients adds up to the growth of a strong nervous system making the kid aware of everything that goes around them.

Kids with high sensitivity will react to everything immediately, learn new things fast, adapt quickly and come out of medical conditions faster than others.

There's so much that a kid with highly sensitive nervous system will do and there's nothing to worry about. It is time for you to enjoy the quick response of your kid because they are quick to grow into an athlete or humans with improved capabilities.

The varied medical conditions, mother's health, medicines consumed and comfort are going to combine and affect the health of your kid during the pregnancy stage. It is always advised to take proper care of the pregnant woman because it is tough to improve the health of a kid who was damaged during the pregnancy. Do not compromise with the health of your kid, provide pregnant ladies with the best of comfort, medical attention and other nutrients necessary for the growth of a healthy baby.

Cognitive Development of Toddlers and Young Kids

In the growing years, it is important to ensure that a kid develops the cognitive skills in the early years of their life, skills such as memory, attention, thinking ability, reasoning ability and the like. The early years of a kid's life generally referred, in this case, is from the time of birth to the age of 5 or 6. These cognitive skills would also include reading, language, vocabulary and numeracy skills.

As per a lot of scientific studies, kids pick up a huge amount of language and vocabulary right in the first year of their life even before they start forming whole sentences. Most babies if provided the correct environment are able to figure out the right words, their tempo and rhythm even before they utter their first word.

The importance of cognitive development in the early years and the knowledge and understanding of the alphabets in the kindergarten stage can predict a kid's reading and learning ability right till the tenth grade of their education. Even though many would not understand the fact, the process of learning words and languages for a kid starts right from the first day of their life.

As the early years are very important in developing a kid's overall mental growth, it is very important to teach them right. A kid grabs and learns words and sentences very quickly, so you need to provide the right environment and literacy interactions and ample opportunities to your kid to learn and grow.

The building blocks of learning and developing skills of reading can be developed only if the right kind of atmosphere has been provided to them. If a child enters kindergarten without learning these skills, it might be very difficult for the kid to cope with the curriculum and keep up with their peers.

Parents are the most crucial and important teachers for kids even before they go to schools. It is very important for parents or caregivers to provide correct kind of care to kids at the early stage of life and provide them with a very cognitive learning environment which are determining factors as to how they would do it the later years and what kind of person or student they would be in the later years of their lives. The proper care for children might give them a head start in the learning years of their life.

There are various organizations which are catering to the basic requirements of parents and caregivers in supporting the kid in the developmental years and helping them raise their babies by providing them information regarding the developmental years and methods of development as a child. The caregiver for kids in the early years should have basic knowledge about the requirements of kids and their different stages of cognitive development along with their requirements in each of those stages. Providing them with an interactive environment at the early stages is very important.

People might think that toys are just an accessory that a kid needs to spend their time or mess around in the early ages of their life but not many are aware of the importance of these toys in the initial years of a baby's life.

Colors are very important to give positivity to a kid's life right from the start. Choosing toys and activities for babies and toddlers might be a very challenging task altogether. One must choose the activities and toys for toddlers very judiciously so that they are able to make the right impression on the kid's mind and make the best out of the whole developmental process for the kid. This job can be very challenging even for the most experienced teachers.

Basic things to keep in mind while choosing toys and activities for babies and toddlers

There are a few basic things which need to be kept in mind while choosing the activities, games, and toys for kids and speed up their developmental process altogether. Some of those things include:

- The age of the baby

This could be as simple as asking a 2-year kid to say tables. It is beyond their scope of syllabi. One must choose the activities and developmental steps on the basis of the kid's age, not taking too much on the platter at a time.

- Mental growth

Not all kids will grow at the same rate mentally even in the starting ages. So even if one should start from a standard basic process of choosing activities, the next set of activities might be different from one kid to another. Each kid might have a different set of needs and requirements in terms of learning and cognitive growth which can be made only with the correct set of choices of activities.

- The requirement of the kid

Different kids have different requirements and hence the kinds of activities to be selected for each one of them also changes as per the same.

As already clear, there is a very strong connection between development and the kind of toys and activities that a kid goes through in the very early age of their lives. Playing is the first most concrete mechanism by which a kid can perceive the world around them and start learning more about the environment they are in.

The different toys will help them learn different cognitive skills and a teacher-child relationship and the right selection of toys by the teachers are very important to expedite the growth of the kid right from the start. A teacher by their experience can make a lot of difference in a kid's development and add meaning to the whole experience of the kid. They are also very important in nurturing the exploring nature of the kids.

The selection of these toys by parents, teachers, and caregivers are very crucial. These toys might be very simple things but they are a part of a continuous learning cycle. Through the games, they form new experiences and these new experiences lead to a connection with their previous ones and thus help them attain an overall growth.

Teachers need to clear about the requirement of the kid and take into account the interest of the kid. For example, if the kid shows any particular interest to colors, the teacher can incorporate the colors to the play blocks and make it even more interacting and engaging for the kid.

These customized toys might help and prove to be an added advantage in the kid's growth and motor, emotional and cognitive development and help the kid to be aware and understand the surrounding faster and better.

There are a number of stages of child development and each one of them is very important and needs special care and recognition. The developmental stages include:

- Language development

In this stage, the kid starts to understand the words spoken to him or her and starts joining sounds and making words of their own. They start understanding their language at this phase.

- Fine motor and gross motor development

In this phase, the overall motor development of the kid takes place.

- Social development

The kid starts to understand the relationships around him or her and starts figuring out what role each one of them have in the society as well as in their lives.

- Emotional development

 The kid forms a strong bond with the parents. This bond plays a very important role in the kid's future.

- Cognitive development

The overall development of the kid as a social being takes place as a whole and the kid starts perceiving the surrounding and becomes aware of the environment and the different kinds of people around them. Cognitive development also involves the thinking and the reasoning skills of the people. Toys can play a very important role in practicing different cognitive skills for kids.

- Mobile

Moving items can attract a child's attention, it can be used to develop the hand-eye coordination of the baby. Hand moving items in stings from above and let the kid try to reach out to it or bat it. These activities might help them understand cause and effect and make an idea about sound and texture.

- Floating objects in a bottle

This, again, is a different form of mobile activity. In a soda bottle, add different small items and secure the cap tightly. Hand it over to the kid and allow him or her to shake it while they look at the different items of interest in the bottle. This also helps to develop the skill of intentionality as well as help them understand the cause and effect relationship.

- Knock-Knock

Create a box-like structure and make different doors like opening on it. Each one might be of a different color of and might have a different shape. Hide an item behind each door, it could be photos or glued objects. Ask the kid to knock on each door to reveal an item and ask them to name it. This develops the naming skills of the kid, helps them learn object permanence as well as understand cause and effect.

- Books

Different pictured books or coloring books might also help in the development of your kid. These are fun and also help to develop a connection between the parents and the kid. Books are fun ways to develop early literacy, learning, and vocabulary, the prediction as well as questioning skills.

- Puppets

Puppets are a good way of teaching kids to imagine, abstract thinking, language and sequencing.

Choosing a toy might not sound like a very challenging task but it actually is very challenging and it depends on a number of factors as well. Choosing the right toy for your baby would decide a number of things for the baby's future and its growth. There are a number of factors to consider while choosing toys for your baby. The basic factors to consider while choosing from thousands of toys are:

- Age of the baby

The age of the baby should be kept in mind while selecting the gift for the baby. With age, the requirement for the gift keeps on changing. A baby's acceptance power increases with age and thus the complication of the toys should increase with age as well to allow an overall cognitive development at that particular age.

- Variety of toys

The same kind of toys might make things monotonous and boring for the baby. Having an assortment of toys each of which is designed individually to have an all-round development should be bought for the baby. Different colors, shapes, and sizes can be considered while buying gifts for the baby. Even a variety of textures can be added to the toys for the baby. These might help the baby to develop sensory as well as motor reflexes.

- Correct stimulation

The right toy will have the right kind of stimulation for the baby. Each individual toy might stimulate a particular of a couple of sense of the baby which may include, touch, sound, taste or sight. It will also help to develop motor and sensory reflexes, hand-eye coordination and a lot more.

- Simplicity

The simplicity of the toys should be taken into consideration. The simpler the toys are, the more profound its effects can be as a baby and longer it can be used in terms of durability. The versatile nature of the toys increases with increasing simplicity of the toy.

- Safety

Safety is the last and the most important factor to be considered while choosing a toy for your baby. While buying a toy, you must ensure that the toy should be safe to use for the baby. There should be absolutely no chance for the toy to cause any harm to the baby, for example, it should be large enough to prevent the baby from choking on it and so on.

Choose the toy for your baby and let them play with it in any way they want to. Always keep in mind that there is no right way to play with a particular toy each child creates its own learning path.

So, if you are particularly stressed and no matter what but playing peekaboo continuously is adding to your exhaustion, then you might want to look at a few creative ideas which will not only break the monotony but also interest your baby. Given below are several objects that are engaging and fun and make really creative playthings for your baby.

- Rainbow Color Drop

This might just involve a drop in a bucket or a box but it's really fun. You can paint small disks or use any different colored balls or marbles or and ask your baby to drop a particular color in an empty wipes box or a bigger bucket. This will prove to be a learning opportunity, helping your baby to identify the different colors and also enhance your baby's hand-eye coordination as he or she learns to find and drop the right colored object in the box.

- Ribbon Pull Play

Creating the structure for this particular game might be a little time consuming but the end product is really appealing and fun for your baby and it will not only help develop motor skills but also create a complete sensory experience as your baby tries to pull and play with the different colored ribbons that you use in creating the toy.

- Splish Splash

This game is perfect for the hot summer months and also when you are trying to teach your baby how to be on her own. All you need to do is spread a rubber or vinyl cloth on the floor and give your baby a shallow container of water. Give some toy cups and bowls and also maybe a doll that they can wash on their own. Research suggests that water has a calming effect on babies so you can use this game when your baby appears to be stressed or fussy about something.

- Bowl Roll

This might be a simple game but it goes a long way to help your child develop his or hand-eye coordination easily and while having fun. You can use any bowl for this game but metal bowls make it more interesting because they reflect.

- Discovery Bottles

Fill several bottles with different things, from glitter, sequins, colored sand or rice to even shampoo and let your baby guess what is inside by shaking and rolling the bottles, before finally opening and looking inside. This game is fun but keep in mind that it might be rather messy and some objects might not be completely safe for your baby. So, make sure you are using bottles that are not too heavy and will not break easily and also that the contents of the bottles are safe or at least that they do not somehow spill out.

- Baby Bowling

This is another game that you can play at home that will help in the physical coordination and development of your baby. This also involves a bit of recycling. To create the bowling pins, you can use old plastic bottles, covered or painted and any kind of a ball. Your baby will find it fun and slowly develop better aim to knock the pins down.

- High Chair Art

Once your baby is able to sit comfortably on the high chair without your support, try giving some safe, edible play materials like play dough or edible paints and let her explore art by trying all these materials. At this stage, babies have the tendency of putting objects in the mouths, so be careful to provide completely safe, nontoxic, edible materials only to avoid any harm. This will enhance your baby's creativity and all help develop motor skills as she tries to mold the dough or and hand paint.

- Baby Light Bright

Babies are always attracted to bright, shiny object and these fascinate them, increasing their curiosity and that is why this particular DIY game center is so very appealing. This game is very Christmassy and perfect for the holiday season but it's just as fun when played during a different time of the year. All you need is a large storage box and several bright, colored Christmas lights. This game is very engaging and your little one will stay busy trying to create different images with the bright lights.

- Disappearing Act

This is another fun trick that will interest your curious little one. Babies are always very curious and they love trying to find things and figure things out. You can simply hide objects behind some tissue paper and let your baby try and find the object. This will need them to think carefully as they try to trace where the object might have disappeared. Such disappearing tricks are fun and they help in the cognitive development of babies while they have fun trying to figure out where the object is.

- Rock and Roll

If you have a large exercise ball at home, then this game is the perfect opportunity to use it for before you get back to your workouts. An exercise ball can be used at different stages of your baby's developments. At the very infant stage, you can hold her and snuggle while making her sit on top of the ball and gently moving back and forth. A little later, you can place the ball under your baby's tummy and roll her around and once your baby is old enough she can push and play with it on their own.

- Baby Food Jar Pick

Babies often fuss at lunchtimes and this game is designed to help with those periods of time when your baby simply won't settle down. Allow your baby to try and push in toys and then bring them out of food jars while you feed. This way you can also recycle those food jars and your baby stays busy playing and developing those motor skills.

The games mentioned above are all designed to help your baby grow and have fun while learning. But it is important to keep in mind that your baby might not always be interested to play and that's why it's necessary to provide encouragement and also breaks in between play.

When you encourage your baby to do something, the task becomes automatically more important. But also remember, that you should take turns and show her how to play with a new toy, or simply participate with your baby. This not only keeps your baby engaged but also creates a stronger emotional bond.

Ensuring the Safety of Your Newborn

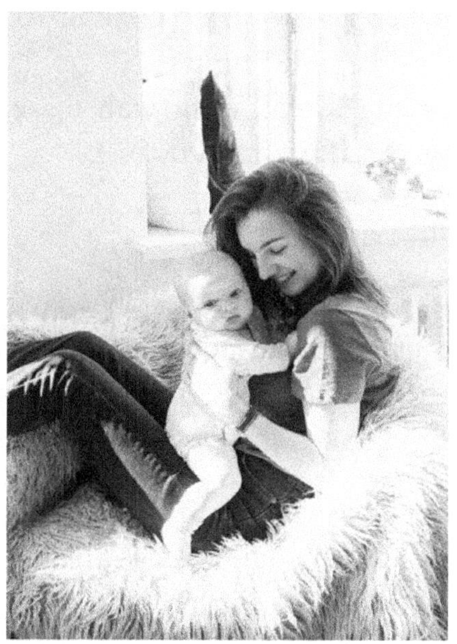

If you are a new parent, it is natural to be all excited the new tiny member of the house. You could be looking for ways to ensure your child's safety and keep them protected. Here are some ideas that could help you take care of your newborn's safety.

- Safety in the car

This is one of the most important aspects of the safety of your newborn child. While this seems like a very obvious thing, a lot of parents go wrong here. First things first, there is a misconception that getting an expensive car seat for your child does the job for you. Unfortunately, that is not the case. As long as any car seat is federally approved for car safety, you are good to go.

There are other factors to consider. For instance, installing it the right way is of the essence. Missing one step from the manual might prove to be quite the issue when it comes to your child's safety.

Next, the ideal position to place your newborn is in the back seat, near the middle, with the child facing the back of the car. It is imperative that you do not sit with the child in your lap while driving the car, even if it is a 5 minute journey. Also, it is best to never place the baby in the passenger seat, even with the car seat intact. This could be rather dangerous for your little one.

- Avoid the falls

Every parent would always complain about their baby falling off a height. This is not uncommon and to some extent, it is absolutely unavoidable. But the idea here is to reduce the chances or possibilities of such falls such that your baby is as safe as possible.

One issue that parents usually face is when they leave the baby carrier on the table and then come back to find the child on the floor. Well, even if you have a baby carrier, it is best never to keep it at a height.

Instead, it would be a better idea to just leave it on the ground. Secondly, leaving your newborn alone on the changing table or bed could also prove to be quite the issue! While you might find it okay to just look away for a few seconds to get a fresh diaper, your baby might just roll and have a fall.

To avoid this, you could just take your child in your arms while you step away to get a diaper. Even if your baby has not started to roll yet, it is better to be safe than sorry!

- Sleeping habits for the newborn

How your child sleeps or where they sleep plays a huge role in ascertaining their safety at home. Even though a lot of parents would not realize this, a child needs a firm mattress to sleep on. Soft mattresses or sofa sets or even couches could actually prove to be quite difficult.

In fact, the time between 2 months and 4 months of age is the most sensitive for the children when it comes to sleeping issues. A firm mattress that is approved for safety should be your only choice for your little one's sleeping area. In addition, they should always be placed on their back during naptime, irrespective of the time of the day.

Apart from that, if your child sleeps in a crib, it is advisable to remove all toys and loose bedding or unnecessary blankets from there. Any of these toys or objects could prove to be a danger for the child. And when the newborn starts to roll on the bed or in the crib, the parents should be extra careful to ensure their safety at this point.

- Poison-proof the house

Poison proofing the house before the birth of your child could be helpful in maintaining the little one's safety. There are a lot of times when the parents do not even realize how the common household goods could prove to be quite a hazard for the newborn.

For instance, medicines lying around in the house is a potential problem here. If the child comes in contact with medicines in the house or consumes them, it could be poisonous for them. Thus, medicines should be locked up at home, inaccessible by the little ones.

Your newborn baby should also not come in contact with detergents and soap that are left loose at home. Keeping them safe in tight containers is of the essence here. Household products like room freshener, tile cleaners, and the likes should also be treated the same way. All of these are actually poisonous for your child. It is best to make a note of these before your little one enters your house.

- Fire safety

Is fire safety really that important for your newborn's safety? Usually, all homes are checked for fire safety; so is it required to check it once the baby is born? These are natural questions. And more often than not, parents just take this type of safety measures for granted.

However, when you bring the little one to your house, it is best to take every precaution to ensure their safety. First and foremost, the golden rule is to never leave your baby alone in any room, even if it is for a few minutes. If an accident were to happen in that period of time, your baby's security and safety would be compromised.

Installing smoke detectors in every floor of your room is of the essence. On top of that, include a separate smoke detector in your child's room. Also, it is a good idea to ensure that your baby's room has a decent window for safety measures. And finally, it is always best to have a solid escape plan in case of a fire. These could include crucial decisions like the escape route to take or how to get the child out in case of emergencies.

Vaccination Guidelines for new-born American Academy of Pediatrics

Newborn kids are at the highest risk of acquiring diseases and infections that can last a lifetime. Polio, hepatitis, and jaundice are some of the most common diseases that can have long-lasting effects. While polio can limit the kid to bed for a life, jaundice, and hepatitis can steal the joy of living.

Governments from around the world have shown concern regarding the eradication of these lethal diseases and have also taken steps to achieve the goals. While governments are continuously striving to secure the lives of these infants, varied private organizations have also let their hands in the eradication of these diseases.

Early vaccination has emerged as the key to protect against polio, jaundice, and hepatitis. Doctors and medical researchers from the remotest corners of the world have voted in favor of earlier vaccination. Today, governments and private agencies are investing billions of dollars in safeguarding the future of infants. Continuous educational campaigns and promotions have educated people about these vaccinations and now people are ensuring that their new-born kids are provided with all of them.

Here's why early vaccination has proven to be so useful:

- Newborns are highly sensitive

After spending 9 months in a secure womb where only the favorable nutrients and elements have reached them, kids are suddenly exposed to viruses and bacteria of all kind. The contemporary world is full of viruses and bacteria, most of them are present in air, making it tough for us to protect our newborns. Since we cannot stop the flow of bacteria in the air, we must rely on strengthening the immune system of our kids.

Physical contact, dirty clothes, unfavorable atmosphere and lack of cleansing are some of the common causes due to which jaundice and hepatitis occur in new-born kids. Keeping kids away from dirty places and contaminated clothes is a good idea but getting the vaccination at the earliest is the best way out.

- Mother's milk can affect the health too

Sometimes Mother's milk can prove to be harmful. The case where mother's milk affects the health of a new-born in a bad manner is dependent upon the overall health of the mother. Excessive of iron, calcium or jaundice viruses can affect the kid's health as well.

Hence, when the kids are vaccinated at the earliest, the risk of acquiring such diseases decreases drastically. With the help of vaccination, the kid's immune system is provided with the requisite strength to fight viruses of varied diseases and survive. A kid being fed with mother's milk without proper vaccination can acquire diseases that will last a lifetime.

- Hepatitis B and Jaundice are the measure concern

Governments and agencies from around the world have reached a consensus that jaundice and hepatitis B are the major concern in newborns. Governments are making it mandatory to provide every new-born with hepatitis B vaccinations within 24 hours of delivery. Proper vaccinations under 24 hours from delivery will ensure that newborn's body acquires the requisite immunity against hepatitis B and jaundice. These two fatal diseases attack the liver and makes it tough for the kid to filter everything they consume leading to liver failure and liver cancer in extreme cases.

What Are The Measures A Mother Should Undertake Before Delivery?

Well! A mother can prevent diseases like polio, jaundice and hepatitis B from affecting her new-born kids like no one else. Since everything the new-born consumes is from her mother's body, it is easier to identify and issues related to health.

A mother must take these steps before delivery to ensure a healthy new-born:

- Get a regular check-up for Hepatitis B and Jaundice

It is proven that the diseases a mother suffers from get transmitted to her kids. You can easily work on those diseases and ensure that it does not get transmitted to your new-born. Get regularly checked for diseases like jaundice and hepatitis B when pregnant. Once, it is known that you are suffering from these diseases, you can provide your kid with vaccination at the earliest and ensure that they develop the requisite strength to fight the virus.

- Avoid oily and greasy food

Even if you are not suffering from hepatitis B during pregnancy but have suffered from either jaundice or hepatitis B in the past, it is advised to avoid oily and greasy food. When you are pregnant, everything you eat affects the health of your kid. Even iron, calcium, and too much protein can harm the kid hence get in touch with your doctor and have a well-crafted diet chart ready by your side for pregnancy period.

Vaccination Guidelines that resonates with the guidelines of the American Academy of Pediatrics

- Vaccination for new-born kids within 24hrs of delivery

The American Academy of Pediatrics advises aggressively to get every new-born vaccinated within 24 hours of delivery. All medical institutions and parents must follow the dictate and ensure that their kid is free of hepatitis B and jaundice.

Vaccination under 24 hours reduces the chances of acquiring infection and diseases like Hepatitis B by advancing the immune system and providing it with the requisite strength to fight varied viruses.

Kids of mothers suffering from Hepatitis B need to be vaccinated immediately: American Academy of Pediatrics coaxes that every kid whose mother is suffering from hepatitis B needs to be vaccinated immediately after birth. Immediate vaccination ensures that no virus or infection occurs related to Hepatitis B through breast feeding.

- For infants with mothers not suffering hepatitis B vaccination under 24 hrs

In case the infant's mother is not Hepatitis B positive, then the vaccination needs to be done within 24 hours of delivery and not immediately after birth. In varied dictates and norms, American Academy of Pediatrics has made it clear that all kinds of vaccination need to be done under 24 hours of delivery no matter what.

What is the American Academy of Pediatrics?

American Academy of Pediatrics aka AAP is popular for its norms that surround the health and vaccination of new-born infants. With other countries joining America in following the guidelines of AAP, the value of this prestigious institution has increased by leaps and bounds. One can easily rely on its guidelines for ensuring that their kid is healthy and free from an attack of varied viruses.

Through varied researches and studies, AAP has found everything related to a newborn's health and these guidelines are the product of those hard work and intricate studies.

More than 60,000 pediatricians and professionals related to health come together to form a society known as the American Academy of Pediatrics. The reputed institution has helped varied governments from around the world in framing a health guideline for newborns as well as pregnant ladies.

Mistakes Most New Parents Are Found Making

Becoming a parent is perhaps one of the most beautiful things on this planet. Giving birth to a baby and nurturing them into a full grown human is perhaps one of the best ways of experiences of life. While everyone who is willing can become a parent but not everyone can become a good parent. Sometimes people are faced with circumstances that force them to be not-so-good parents other times it just the habits that fail them as a parent.

Are you one of those parents who is failing big at parenting? Are you not happy with the way you are managing your newborn's life and schedule? Well, here are a few things you might be doing wrong. You can get on the right track of parenting by making these little changes in your lifestyle:

- Strictly following the book

It is obvious for you to be scared since it's your first baby coaxing you to follow everything written in the good books of parenting. Just when you start following everything written in the book, you start aiming to be perfect, which is impossible to achieve. It is always a good idea to innovate, try new things and do things your way. Do not go by the book even when you know that you can do it differently and you can do it better.

- Stop spending too much on clothing for new-born

Your newborn is going to grow to thrice to its size in coming weeks hence do not waste a lot of money in buying expensive clothing. There's a lot of other things you can spend on and it will make sense. Spending on clothing for new-born is a simple waste of money and time. Buy items that will help the kid grow, become cheerful and helps with entertainment instead of buying expensive clothes.

- Not sleeping when your kid is sleeping

Well, here's an anecdote for all you parents, you cannot afford to not sleep when your kid is sleeping and expect to sleep at night. Every parent must adjust their schedule according to their newborn's sleeping pattern. Sleep when they are asleep and stay awake with them. Do not do all other chores when they are asleep and try to sleep at night when they are awake. Adjusting your sleep timing will require you to have someone who can manage other important chores throughout the day. Ask your parents, cousin or friends for a little help for a few months.

- Comparing your kid with the others

Different mothers, different eating patterns, different kind of body and different genes will give birth to different babies hence it is not okay to compare your new-born with your brother's or sister's kid. Never compare your kids with others because it will only bring disappointment to you. Every kid grows under different conditions in different wombs hence they are not going to be the same. Some will grow fast, some will slow, and some will walk early while some will take a few more months. It is okay to wait and see your kid laugh and run. Do not ruin the moments of your new-born by comparing it with other kids.

- Not preserving the moment

If you think, you will never forget your kid's first laughter, her first walk or his first fall, then you are wrong. We all tend to forget things because we all are busy with our kids in the present. Start maintaining a journal where you can store all the photographs and all the memories that will last a lifetime. Do not rely on your memory that will go haywire with time, leaving you gasping for moments from your kid's childhood. In the technology laden world, it is so easy to record, click and store photos and videos, be a little active with journal maintenance and you will preserve these memories for a lifetime.

- Being overprotective

The only thing that will restrict your baby's growth is you. Do not be overprotective when it comes to walking, running or eating. Let your kid try new things and eat new things. It is only by trying to walk, run or jump that your kid is going to be able to do all of those things. Let them mingle with other kids, do not be scared that they will be harmed or something. A little scratch or wound won't make much of a difference but you being overprotective can ruin your kid's childhood.

- Not asking for help

As a mother or a father the last mistake should be making is not asking for help. It is going to be difficult to continue with your life when you have a baby who wakes up every night only to scream and cry. Ask your cousin, brother, mother or father to walk them around for a bit. Be accepting when someone offers help and also be very open about asking help. Do not be too egoist or proud about nourishing your kid on your own, let it become a family affair.

- Not enjoying your life

Raising a kid is not about a month or two, it's a 15-16 years long affair hence do not miss out on your life. Take your wife out for a ride, a movie or for a dinner. Let your parents handle your kid for a day or two. Go around have fun because these moments are not going to return. You might grow depressed and sad only by catering to the needs of your kid, make time for yourself and your spouse. Take that small gate away and have fun.

Since there's no book that guarantees a perfect parenthood experience, it gets necessary for you to try and learn at the same time.

Learn from the little mistakes you make and do not be afraid to try new things. Remember, someone who wrote a book on parenting was also trying before he or she mastered it.

Conclusion

Nevertheless, parenting is an exciting experience that comes with its own series of ups and downs. Cherish the moments, and enjoy this phase.

The key to happy and successful parenting is to establish a strong bond with your baby, and understand her needs.

We hope this guide would have helped you in clearing your doubts.

Happy parenting!